MRS. DALLOWAY

Virginia Woolf

Spark Educational Publishing
A Division of Barnes & Noble Publishing
120 Fifth Avenue
New York, NY 10011

ISBN 1-4114-0254-5

Please submit all comments and questions or report errors to *www.sparknotes.com/errors*

Printed and bound in the United States

Introduction:
Stopping to Buy SparkNotes on a Snowy Evening

Whose words these are you *think* you know.
Your paper's due tomorrow, though;
We're glad to see you stopping here
To get some help before you go.

Lost your course? You'll find it here.
Face tests and essays without fear.
Between the words, good grades at stake:
Get great results throughout the year.

Once school bells caused your heart to quake
As teachers circled each mistake.
Use SparkNotes and no longer weep,
Ace every single test you take.

Yes, books are lovely, dark, and deep,
But only what you grasp you keep,
With hours to go before you sleep,
With hours to go before you sleep.

Contents

CONTEXT

Virginia Woolf, the English novelist, critic, and essayist, was born on January 25, 1882, to Leslie Stephen, a literary critic, and Julia Duckworth Stephen. Woolf grew up in an upper-middle-class, socially active, literary family in Victorian London. She had three full siblings, two half-brothers, and two half-sisters. She was educated at home, becoming a voracious reader of the books in her father's extensive library. Tragedy first afflicted the family when Woolf's mother died in 1895, then hit again two years later, when her half-sister, Stella, the caregiver in the Stephen family, died. Woolf experienced her first bout of mental illness after her mother's death, and she suffered from mania and severe depression for the rest of her life.

Patriarchal, repressive Victorian society did not encourage women to attend universities or to participate in intellectual debate. Nonetheless, Woolf began publishing her first essays and reviews after 1904, the year her father died and she and her siblings moved to the Bloomsbury area of London. Young students and artists, drawn to the vitality and intellectual curiosity of the Stephen clan, congregated on Thursday evenings to share their views about the world. The Bloomsbury group, as Woolf and her friends came to be called, disregarded the constricting taboos of the Victorian era, and such topics as religion, sex, and art fueled the talk at their weekly salons. They even discussed homosexuality, a subject that shocked many of the group's contemporaries. For Woolf, the group served as the undergraduate education that society had denied her.

The Voyage Out, Woolf's first novel, was published in 1915, three years after her marriage to Leonard Woolf, a member of the Bloomsbury group. Their partnership furthered the group's intellectual ideals. With Leonard, Woolf founded Hogarth Press, which published Sigmund Freud, Katherine Mansfield, T. S. Eliot, and other notable authors. She determinedly pursued her own writing as well: During the next few years, Woolf kept a diary and wrote several novels, a collection of short stories, and numerous essays. She struggled, as she wrote, to both deal with her bouts of bipolarity and to find her true voice as a writer. Before World War I, Woolf viewed the realistic Victorian novel, with its neat and linear plots, as an inadequate form of expression. Her opinion intensified after the war, and in the 1920s she began searching for the form that would reflect the violent contrasts and disjointed impressions of the world around her.

In *Mrs. Dalloway*, published in 1925, Woolf discovered a new literary form capable of expressing the new realities of postwar England. The novel depicts the subjective experiences and memories of its central characters over a single day in post–World War I London. Divided into parts, rather than chapters, the novel's structure highlights the finely interwoven texture of the characters' thoughts. Critics tend to agree that Woolf found her writer's voice with this novel. At forty-three, she knew her experimental style was unlikely to be a popular success but no longer felt compelled to seek critical praise. The novel did, however, gain a measure of commercial and critical success. This book, which focuses on commonplace tasks, such as shopping, throwing a party, and eating dinner, showed that no act was too small or too ordinary for a writer's attention. Ultimately, *Mrs. Dalloway* transformed the novel as an art form.

Woolf develops the book's protagonist, Clarissa Dalloway, and myriad other characters by chronicling their interior thoughts with little pause or explanation, a style referred to as stream of consciousness. Several central characters and more than one hundred minor characters appear in the text, and their thoughts spin out like spider webs. Sometimes the threads of thought cross—and people succeed in communicating. More often, however, the threads do not cross, leaving the characters isolated and alone. Woolf believed that behind the "cotton wool" of life, as she terms it in her autobiographical collection of essays *Moments of Being* (1941), and under the downpour of impressions saturating a mind during each moment, a pattern exists.

Characters in *Mrs. Dalloway* occasionally perceive life's pattern through a sudden shock, or what Woolf called a "moment of being." Suddenly the cotton wool parts, and a person sees reality, and his or her place in it, clearly. "In the vast catastrophe of the European war," wrote Woolf, "our emotions had to be broken up for us, and put at an angle from us, before we could allow ourselves to feel them in poetry or fiction." These words appear in her essay collection, *The Common Reader*, which was published just one month before *Mrs. Dalloway*. Her novel attempts to uncover fragmented emotions, such as desperation or love, in order to find, through "moments of being," a way to endure.

While writing *Mrs. Dalloway*, Woolf reread the Greek classics along with two new modernist writers, Marcel Proust and James

Joyce. Woolf shared these writers' interest in time and psychology, and she incorporated these issues into her novel. She wanted to show characters in flux, rather than static, characters who think and emote as they move through space, who react to their surroundings in ways that mirrored actual human experience. Rapid political and social change marked the period between the two world wars: the British Empire, for which so many people had sacrificed their lives to protect and preserve, was in decline. Countries like India were beginning to question Britain's colonial rule. At home, the Labour Party, with its plans for economic reform, was beginning to challenge the Conservative Party, with its emphasis on imperial business interests. Women, who had flooded the workforce to replace the men who had gone to war, were demanding equal rights. Men, who had seen unspeakable atrocities in the first modern war, were questioning the usefulness of class-based sociopolitical institutions. Woolf lent her support to the feminist movement in her nonfiction book *A Room of One's Own* (1929), as well as in numerous essays, and she was briefly involved in the women's suffrage movement. Although *Mrs. Dalloway* portrays the shifting political atmosphere through the characters Peter Walsh, Richard Dalloway, and Hugh Whitbread, it focuses more deeply on the charged social mood through the characters Septimus Warren Smith and Clarissa Dalloway. Woolf delves into the consciousness of Clarissa, a woman who exists largely in the domestic sphere, to ensure that readers take her character seriously, rather than simply dismiss her as a vain and uneducated upper-class wife. In spite of her heroic and imperfect effort in life, Clarissa, like every human being and even the old social order itself, must face death.

Woolf's struggles with mental illness gave her an opportunity to witness firsthand how insensitive medical professionals could be, and she critiques their tactlessness in *Mrs. Dalloway*. One of Woolf's doctors suggested that plenty of rest and rich food would lead to a full recovery, a cure prescribed in the novel, and another removed several of her teeth. In the early twentieth century, mental health problems were too often considered imaginary, an embarrassment, or the product of moral weakness. During one bout of illness, Woolf heard birds sing like Greek choruses and King Edward use foul language among some azaleas. In 1941, as England entered a second world war, and at the onset of another breakdown she feared would be permanent, Woolf placed a large stone in her pocket to weigh herself down and drowned herself in the River Ouse.

PLOT OVERVIEW

Mrs. *Dalloway* covers one day from morning to night in one woman's life. Clarissa Dalloway, an upper-class housewife, walks through her London neighborhood to prepare for the party she will host that evening. When she returns from flower shopping, an old suitor and friend, Peter Walsh, drops by her house unexpectedly. The two have always judged each other harshly, and their meeting in the present intertwines with their thoughts of the past. Years earlier, Clarissa refused Peter's marriage proposal, and Peter has never quite gotten over it. Peter asks Clarissa if she is happy with her husband, Richard, but before she can answer, her daughter, Elizabeth, enters the room. Peter leaves and goes to Regent's Park. He thinks about Clarissa's refusal, which still obsesses him.

The point of view then shifts to Septimus, a veteran of World War I who was injured in trench warfare and now suffers from shell shock. Septimus and his Italian wife, Lucrezia, pass time in Regent's Park. They are waiting for Septimus's appointment with Sir William Bradshaw, a celebrated psychiatrist. Before the war, Septimus was a budding young poet and lover of Shakespeare; when the war broke out, he enlisted immediately for romantic patriotic reasons. He became numb to the horrors of war and its aftermath: when his friend Evans died, he felt little sadness. Now Septimus sees nothing of worth in the England he fought for, and he has lost the desire to preserve either his society or himself. Suicidal, he believes his lack of feeling is a crime. Clearly Septimus's experiences in the war have permanently scarred him, and he has serious mental problems. However, Sir William does not listen to what Septimus says and diagnoses "a lack of proportion." Sir William plans to separate Septimus from Lucrezia and send him to a mental institution in the country.

Richard Dalloway eats lunch with Hugh Whitbread and Lady Bruton, members of high society. The men help Lady Bruton write a letter to the *Times*, London's largest newspaper. After lunch, Richard returns home to Clarissa with a large bunch of roses. He intends to tell her that he loves her but finds that he cannot, because it has been so long since he last said it. Clarissa considers the void that exists between people, even between husband and wife. Even though she values the privacy she is able to maintain in her marriage, considering it vital to the success of the relationship, at the same time she finds slightly disturbing the fact that Richard doesn't know everything about her. Clarissa sees off Elizabeth and her history teacher, Miss Kilman, who are going shopping. The two older women despise one another passionately, each believing the other to be an oppressive force over Elizabeth. Meanwhile, Septimus and Lucrezia are in their apartment, enjoying a moment of happiness together before the men come to take Septimus to the asylum. One of Septimus's doctors, Dr. Holmes, arrives, and Septimus fears the doctor will destroy his soul. In order to avoid this fate, he jumps from a window to his death.

Peter hears the ambulance go by to pick up Septimus's body and marvels ironically at the level of London's civilization. He goes to Clarissa's party, where most of the novel's major characters are assembled. Clarissa works hard to make her party a success but feels dissatisfied by her own role and acutely conscious of Peter's critical eye. All the partygoers, but especially Peter and Sally Seton, have, to some degree, failed to accomplish the dreams of their youth. Though the social order is undoubtedly changing, Elizabeth and the members of her generation will probably repeat the errors of Clarissa's generation. Sir William Bradshaw arrives late, and his wife explains that one of his patients, the young veteran (Septimus), has committed suicide. Clarissa retreats to the privacy of a small room to consider Septimus's death. She understands that he was overwhelmed by life and that men like Sir William make life intolerable. She identifies with Septimus, admiring him for having taken the plunge and for not compromising his soul. She feels, with her comfortable position as a society hostess, responsible for his death. The party nears its close as guests begin to leave. Clarissa enters the room, and her presence fills Peter with a great excitement.

CHARACTER LIST

Clarissa Dalloway The eponymous protagonist. The novel begins with Clarissa's point of view and follows her perspective more closely than that of any other character. As Clarissa prepares for the party she will give that evening, we are privy to her meandering thoughts. Clarissa is vivacious and cares a great deal about what people think of her, but she is also self-reflective. She often questions life's true meaning, wondering whether happiness is truly possible. She feels both a great joy and a great dread about her life, both of which manifest in her struggles to strike a balance between her desire for privacy and her need to communicate with others. Throughout the day Clarissa reflects on the crucial summer when she chose to marry her husband, Richard, instead of her friend Peter Walsh. Though she is happy with Richard, she is not entirely certain she made the wrong choice about Peter, and she also thinks frequently about her friend Sally Seton, whom she also once loved.

Septimus Warren Smith A World War I veteran suffering from shell shock, married to an Italian woman named Lucrezia. Though he is insane, Septimus views English society in much the same way as Clarissa does, and he struggles, as she does, to both maintain his privacy and fulfill his need to communicate with others. He shares so many traits with Clarissa that he could be her double. Septimus is pale, has a hawklike posture, and wears a shabby overcoat. Before the war he was a young, idealistic, aspiring poet. After the war he regards human nature as evil and believes he is guilty of not being able to feel. Rather than succumb to the society he abhors, he commits suicide.

Peter Walsh A close friend of Clarissa's, once desperately in love with her. Clarissa rejected Peter's marriage proposal when she was eighteen, and he moved to India. He has not been to London for five years. He is highly critical of others, is conflicted about nearly everything in his life, and has a habit of playing with his pocketknife. Often overcome with emotion, he cries easily. He frequently has romantic problems with women and is currently in love with Daisy, a married woman in India. He wears horn-rimmed glasses and a bow tie and used to be a Socialist.

Sally Seton A close friend of Clarissa and Peter in their youth. Sally was a wild, handsome ragamuffin who smoked cigars and would say anything. She and Clarissa were sexually attracted to one another as teenagers. Now Sally lives in Manchester and is married with five boys. Her married name is Lady Rosseter.

Richard Dalloway Clarissa's husband. A member of Parliament in the Conservative government, Richard plans to write a history of the great English military family, the Brutons, when the Labour Party comes to power. He is a sportsman and likes being in the country. He is a loving father and husband. While devoted to social reform, he appreciates English tradition. He has failed to make it into the Cabinet, or main governing body.

Hugh Whitbread Clarissa's old friend, married to Evelyn Whitbread. An impeccable Englishman and upholder of English tradition, Hugh writes letters to the *Times* about various causes. He never brushes beneath the surface of any subject and is rather vain. Many are critical of his pompousness and gluttony, but he remains oblivious. He is, as Clarissa thinks, almost too perfectly dressed. He makes Clarissa feel young and insecure.

Lucrezia Smith (Rezia) Septimus's wife, a twenty-four-year-old hat-maker from Milan. Rezia loves Septimus but is forced to bear the burden of his mental illness alone. Normally a lively and playful young woman, she has grown thin with worry. She feels isolated and continually wishes to share her unhappiness with somebody. She trims hats for the friends of her neighbor, Mrs. Filmer.

Elizabeth Dalloway Clarissa and Richard's only child. Gentle, considerate, and somewhat passive, seventeen-year-old Elizabeth does not have Clarissa's energy. She has a dark beauty that is beginning to attract attention. Not a fan of parties or clothes, she likes being in the country with her father and dogs. She spends a great deal of time praying with her history teacher, the religious Miss Kilman, and is considering career options.

Doris Kilman Elizabeth's history teacher, who has German ancestry. Miss Kilman has a history degree and was fired from a teaching job during the war because of society's anti-German prejudice. She is over forty and wears an unattractive mackintosh coat because she does not dress to please. She became a born-again Christian two years and three months ago. Poor, with a forehead like an egg, she is bitter and dislikes Clarissa intensely but adores Elizabeth.

Sir William Bradshaw A renowned London psychiatrist. When Lucrezia seeks help for her insane husband, Septimus, Septimus's doctor, Dr. Holmes, recommends Sir William. Sir William believes that most people who think they are mad suffer instead from a "lack of proportion." He determines that Septimus has suffered a complete nervous breakdown and recommends that Septimus spend time in the country, apart from Lucrezia. The hardworking son of a tradesman, Sir William craves power and has become respected in his field.

Dr. Holmes Septimus's general practitioner. When Septimus begins to suffer the delayed effects of shell shock, Lucrezia seeks his help. Dr. Holmes claims nothing is wrong with Septimus, but that Lucrezia should see Sir William if she doesn't believe him. Septimus despises Dr. Holmes and refers to him as "human nature." Dr. Holmes likes to go to the music hall and to play golf.

Lady (Millicent) Bruton A member of high society and a friend of the Dalloways. At sixty-two years old, Lady Bruton is devoted to promoting emigration to Canada for English families. Normally erect and magisterial, she panics when she has to write a letter to the editor and seeks help from Richard Dalloway and Hugh Whitbread. She has an assistant, Milly Brush, and a chow dog. She is a descendant of General Sir Talbot Moore.

Miss Helena Parry (Aunt Helena) Clarissa's aunt. Aunt Helena is a relic of the strict English society Clarissa finds so confining. A great botanist, she also enjoys talking about orchids and Burma. She is a formidable old lady, over eighty, who found Sally Seton's behavior as a youth shocking. She has one glass eye.

Ellie Henderson Clarissa's dowdy cousin. Ellie, in her early fifties, has thin hair, a meager profile, and bad eyesight. Not trained for any career and having only a small income, she wears an old black dress to Clarissa's party. She is self-effacing, subject to chills, and close to a woman named Edith. Clarissa finds her dull and does not want to invite her to the party, and Ellie stands alone nearly the whole time, aware that she does not really belong.

Evans Septimus's wartime officer and close friend. Evans died in Italy just before the armistice, but Septimus, in his deluded state, continues to see and hear him behind trees and sitting room screens. During the war, Evans and Septimus were inseparable. Evans was a shy Englishman with red hair.

Mrs. Filmer The Smiths' neighbor. Mrs. Filmer finds Septimus odd. She has honest blue eyes and is Rezia's only friend in London. Her daughter is Mrs. Peters, who listens to the Smiths' gramophone when they are not at home. Mrs. Filmer's granddaughter delivers the newspaper to the Smiths' home each evening, and Rezia always makes the child's arrival into a momentous, joyous event.

Daisy Simmons Peter Walsh's lover in India, married to a major in the Indian army. Daisy is twenty-four years old and has two small children. Peter is in London to arrange her divorce.

Evelyn Whitbread Hugh Whitbread's wife. Evelyn suffers from an unspecified internal ailment and spends much of her time in nursing homes. We learn about her from others. Peter Walsh describes her as mousy and almost negligible, but he also points out that occasionally she says something sharp.

Mr. Brewer Septimus's boss at Sibleys and Arrowsmith. Mr. Brewer, the managing clerk, is paternal with his employees and foresees a promising career for Septimus, but Septimus volunteers for the war before he can reach any degree of success. Mr. Brewer promotes Septimus when he returns from the war, but Septimus is already losing his mind. Mr. Brewer has a waxed moustache and a coral tiepin.

Jim Hutton An awful poet at the Dalloways' party. Jim is badly dressed, with red socks and unruly hair, and he does not enjoy talking to another guest, Professor Brierly, who is a professor of Milton. Jim shares with Clarissa a love of Bach and thinks she is "the best of the great ladies who took an interest in art." He enjoys mimicking people.

ANALYSIS OF MAJOR CHARACTERS

CLARISSA DALLOWAY

Clarissa Dalloway, the heroine of the novel, struggles constantly to balance her internal life with the external world. Her world consists of glittering surfaces, such as fine fashion, parties, and high society, but as she moves through that world she probes beneath those surfaces in search of deeper meaning. Yearning for privacy, Clarissa has a tendency toward introspection that gives her a profound capacity for emotion, which many other characters lack. However, she is always concerned with appearances and keeps herself tightly composed, seldom sharing her feelings with anyone. She uses a constant stream of convivial chatter and activity to keep her soul locked safely away, which can make her seem shallow even to those who know her well.

Constantly overlaying the past and the present, Clarissa strives to reconcile herself to life despite her potent memories. For most of the novel she considers aging and death with trepidation, even as she performs life-affirming actions, such as buying flowers. Though content, Clarissa never lets go of the doubt she feels about the decisions that have shaped her life, particularly her decision to marry Richard instead of Peter Walsh. She understands that life with Peter would have been difficult, but at the same time she is uneasily aware that she sacrificed passion for the security and tranquility of an upper-class life. At times she wishes for a chance to live life over again. She experiences a moment of clarity and peace when she watches her old neighbor through her window, and by the end of the day she has come to terms with the possibility of death. Like Septimus, Clarissa feels keenly the oppressive forces in life, and she accepts that the life she has is all she'll get. Her will to endure, however, prevails.

SEPTIMUS WARREN SMITH

Septimus, a veteran of World War I, suffers from shell shock and is lost within his own mind. He feels guilty even as he despises himself for being made numb by the war. His doctor has ordered Lucrezia, Septimus's wife, to make Septimus notice things outside himself, but Septimus has removed himself from the physical world. Instead, he lives in an internal world, wherein he sees and hears things that aren't really there and he talks to his dead friend Evans. He is sometimes overcome with the beauty in the world, but he also fears that the people in it have no capacity for honesty or kindness. Woolf intended for Clarissa to speak the sane truth and Septimus the insane truth, and indeed Septimus's detachment enables him to judge other people more harshly than Clarissa is capable of. The world outside of Septimus is threatening, and the way Septimus sees that world offers little hope.

On the surface, Septimus seems quite dissimilar to Clarissa, but he embodies many characteristics that Clarissa shares and thinks in much the same way she does. He could almost be her double in the novel. Septimus and Clarissa both have beak-noses, love Shakespeare, and fear oppression. More important, as Clarissa's double, Septimus offers a contrast between the conscious struggle of a working-class veteran and the blind opulence of the upper class. His troubles call into question the legitimacy of the English society he fought to preserve during the war. Because his thoughts often run parallel to Clarissa's and echo hers in many ways, the thin line between what is considered sanity and insanity gets thinner and thinner. Septimus chooses to escape his problems by killing himself, a dramatic and tragic gesture that ultimately helps Clarissa to accept her own choices, as well as the society in which she lives.

PETER WALSH

Peter Walsh's most consistent character trait is ambivalence: he is middle-aged and fears he has wasted his life, but sometimes he also feels he is not yet old. He cannot commit to an identity, or even to a romantic partner. He cannot decide what he feels and tries often to talk himself into feeling or not feeling certain things. For example, he spends the day telling himself that he no longer loves Clarissa, but his grief at losing her rises painfully to the surface when he is in her presence, and his obsession with her suggests that he is still attracted to her and may even long for renewed romance. Even when he gathers his anger toward Clarissa and tells her about his new love, he cannot sustain the anger and ends up weeping. Peter acts as a foil to Richard, who is stable, generous, and rather simple. Unlike calm

Richard, Peter is like a storm, thundering and crashing, unpredictable even to himself.

Peter's unhealed hurt and persistent insecurity make him severely critical of other characters, especially the Dalloways. He detests Clarissa's bourgeois lifestyle, though he blames Richard for making her into the kind of woman she is. Clarissa intuits even his most veiled criticisms, such as when he remarks on her green dress, and his judgments strongly affect her own assessments of her life and choices. Despite his sharp critiques of others, Peter cannot clearly see his own shortcomings. His self-obsession and neediness would have suffocated Clarissa, which is partly why she refused his marriage proposal as a young woman. Peter acquiesces to the very English society he criticizes, enjoying the false sense of order it offers, which he lacks in his life. Despite Peter's ambivalence and tendency toward analysis, he still feels life deeply. While Clarissa comes to terms with her own mortality, Peter becomes frantic at the thought of death. He follows a young woman through the London streets to smother his thoughts of death with a fantasy of life and adventure. His critical nature may distance him from others, but he values his life nonetheless.

SALLY SETON

Sally Seton exists only as a figure in Clarissa's memory for most of the novel, and when she appears at Clarissa's party, she is older but still familiar. Though the women have not seen each other for years, Sally still puts Clarissa first when she counts her blessings, even before her husband or five sons. As a girl, Sally was without inhibitions, and as an adult at the party, she is still effusive and lacks Clarissa's restraint. Long ago, Sally and Clarissa plotted to reform the world together. Now, however, both are married, a fate they once considered a "catastrophe." Sally has changed and calmed down a great deal since the Bourton days, but she is still enough of a loose cannon to make Peter nervous and to kindle Clarissa's old warm feelings. Both Sally and Clarissa have yielded to the forces of English society to some degree, but Sally keeps more distance than Clarissa does. She often takes refuge in her garden, as she despairs over communicating with humans. However, she has not lost all hope of meaningful communication, and she still thinks saying what one feels is the most important contribution one can make to society.

CHARACTER ANALYSIS

Clarissa considers the moment when Sally kissed her on the lips and offered her a flower at Bourton the "most exquisite moment of her whole life." Society would never have allowed that love to flourish, since women of Clarissa's class were expected to marry and become society wives. Sally has always been more of a free spirit than Clarissa, and when she arrives at Clarissa's party, she feels rather distant from and confused by the life Clarissa has chosen. The women's kiss marked a true moment of passion that could have pushed both women outside of the English society they know, and it stands out in contrast to the confrontation Peter remembers between Sally and Hugh regarding women's rights. One morning at Bourton, Sally angrily told Hugh he represented the worst of the English middle class and that he was to blame for the plight of the young girls in Piccadilly. Later, Hugh supposedly kissed her in the smoking room. Hugh's is the forced kiss of traditional English society, while the kiss with Clarissa is a revelation. Ultimately, the society that spurs Hugh's kiss prevails for both women.

RICHARD DALLOWAY

Richard's simplicity and steadfastness have enabled him to build a stable life for Clarissa, but these same qualities represent the compromise that marrying him required. Richard is a simple, hardworking, sensible husband who loves Clarissa and their daughter, Elizabeth. However, he will never share Clarissa's desire to truly and fully communicate, and he cannot appreciate the beauty of life in the same way she can. At one point, Richard tries to overcome his habitual stiffness and shyness by planning to tell Clarissa that he loves her, but he is ultimately too repressed to say the words, in part because it has been so long since he last said them. Just as he does not understand Clarissa's desires, he does not recognize Elizabeth's potential as a woman. If he had had a son, he would have encouraged him to work, but he does not offer the same encouragement to Elizabeth, even as she contemplates job options. His reticence on the matter increases the likelihood that she will eventually be in the same predicament as Clarissa, unable to support herself through a career and thus unable to gain the freedom to follow her passions.

Richard considers tradition of prime importance, rather than passion or open communication. He champions the traditions England went to war to preserve, in contrast to Septimus, and does not recognize their destructive power. Despite his occasional misgivings, Richard has close associations with members of English high society. He is critical of Hugh, but they revere many of the same symbols, including the figure of the grand old lady with money, who is helpless when it comes to surviving in a patriarchal society. Richard likes the fact that women need him, but sometimes he wrongly assumes they do. For example, he does not recognize that a female vagrant may not want his help but may instead enjoy living outside the rules of his society. For Richard, this sort of freedom is unimaginable.

CHARACTER ANALYSIS

THEMES, MOTIFS, AND SYMBOLS

THEMES

Themes are the fundamental and often universal ideas explored in a literary work.

COMMUNICATION VS. PRIVACY

Throughout *Mrs. Dalloway*, Clarissa, Septimus, Peter, and others struggle to find outlets for communication as well as adequate privacy, and the balance between the two is difficult for all to attain. Clarissa in particular struggles to open the pathway for communication and throws parties in an attempt to draw people together. At the same time, she feels shrouded within her own reflective soul and thinks the ultimate human mystery is how she can exist in one room while the old woman in the house across from hers exists in another. Even as Clarissa celebrates the old woman's independence, she knows it comes with an inevitable loneliness. Peter tries to explain the contradictory human impulses toward privacy and communication by comparing the soul to a fish that swims along in murky water, then rises quickly to the surface to frolic on the waves. The war has changed people's ideas of what English society should be, and understanding is difficult between those who support traditional English society and those who hope for continued change. Meaningful connections in this disjointed postwar world are not easy to make, no matter what efforts the characters put forth. Ultimately, Clarissa sees Septimus's death as a desperate, but legitimate, act of communication.

DISILLUSIONMENT WITH THE BRITISH EMPIRE

Throughout the nineteenth century, the British Empire seemed invincible. It expanded into many other countries, such as India, Nigeria, and South Africa, becoming the largest empire the world had ever seen. World War I was a violent reality check. For the first time in nearly a century, the English were vulnerable on their own land. The Allies technically won the war, but the extent of devastation England suffered made it a victory in name only. Entire communities of young men were injured and killed. In 1916, at the Battle of the Somme, England suffered 60,000 casualties—the largest slaughter in England's history. Not surprisingly, English citizens lost much of their faith in the empire after the war. No longer could England claim to be invulnerable and all-powerful. Citizens were less inclined to willingly adhere to the rigid constraints imposed by England's class system, which benefited only a small margin of society but which all classes had fought to preserve.

In 1923, when *Mrs. Dalloway* takes place, the old establishment and its oppressive values are nearing their end. English citizens, including Clarissa, Peter, and Septimus, feel the failure of the empire as strongly as they feel their own personal failures. Those citizens who still champion English tradition, such as Aunt Helena and Lady Bruton, are old. Aunt Helena, with her glass eye (perhaps a symbol of her inability or unwillingness to see the empire's disintegration), is turning into an artifact. Anticipating the end of the Conservative Party's reign, Richard plans to write the history of the great British military family, the Brutons, who are already part of the past. The old empire faces an imminent demise, and the loss of the traditional and familiar social order leaves the English at loose ends.

The Fear of Death

Thoughts of death lurk constantly beneath the surface of everyday life in *Mrs. Dalloway*, especially for Clarissa, Septimus, and Peter, and this awareness makes even mundane events and interactions meaningful, sometimes even threatening. At the very start of her day, when she goes out to buy flowers for her party, Clarissa remembers a moment in her youth when she suspected a terrible event would occur. Big Ben tolls out the hour, and Clarissa repeats a line from Shakespeare's *Cymbeline* over and over as the day goes on: "Fear no more the heat o' the sun / Nor the furious winter's rages." The line is from a funeral song that celebrates death as a comfort after a difficult life. Middle-aged Clarissa has experienced the deaths of her father, mother, and sister and has lived through the calamity of war, and she has grown to believe that living even one day is dangerous. Death is very naturally in her thoughts, and the line from *Cymbeline*, along with Septimus's suicidal embrace of death, ultimately helps her to be at peace with her own mortality. Peter Walsh, so insecure in his identity, grows frantic at the idea of death and follows an anonymous young woman through London to forget about it. Septimus faces death most directly. Though he fears it, he finally chooses it over what seems to him a direr alternative—living another day.

THE THREAT OF OPPRESSION

Oppression is a constant threat for Clarissa and Septimus in *Mrs. Dalloway*, and Septimus dies in order to escape what he perceives to be an oppressive social pressure to conform. It comes in many guises, including religion, science, or social convention. Miss Kilman and Sir William Bradshaw are two of the major oppressors in the novel: Miss Kilman dreams of felling Clarissa in the name of religion, and Sir William would like to subdue all those who challenge his conception of the world. Both wish to convert the world to their belief systems in order to gain power and dominate others, and their rigidity oppresses all who come into contact with them. More subtle oppressors, even those who do not intend to, do harm by supporting the repressive English social system. Though Clarissa herself lives under the weight of that system and often feels oppressed by it, her acceptance of patriarchal English society makes her, in part, responsible for Septimus's death. Thus she too is an oppressor of sorts. At the end of the novel, she reflects on his suicide: "Somehow it was her disaster—her disgrace." She accepts responsibility, though other characters are equally or more fully to blame, which suggests that everyone is in some way complicit in the oppression of others.

MOTIFS

Motifs are recurring structures, contrasts, or literary devices that can help to develop and inform the text's major themes.

TIME

Time imparts order to the fluid thoughts, memories, and encounters that make up *Mrs. Dalloway*. Big Ben, a symbol of England and its might, sounds out the hour relentlessly, ensuring that the passage of time, and the awareness of eventual death, is always palpable. Clarissa, Septimus, Peter, and other characters are in the grip of time, and as they age they evaluate how they have spent their lives. Clarissa, in particular, senses the passage of time, and the appearance of Sally and Peter, friends from the past, emphasizes how much time has gone by since Clarissa was young. Once the hour chimes, however, the sound disappears—its "leaden circles dissolved in the air." This expression recurs many times throughout the novel, indicating how ephemeral time is, despite the pomp of Big Ben and despite people's wary obsession with it. "It is time," Rezia says to Septimus as they sit in the park waiting for the doctor's appointment on Harley Street. The ancient woman at the Regent's Park Tube station suggests that the human condition knows no boundaries of time, since she continues to sing the same song for what seems like eternity. She understands that life is circular, not merely linear, which is the only sort of time that Big Ben tracks. Time is so important to the themes, structure, and characters of this novel that Woolf almost named her book *The Hours*.

SHAKESPEARE

The many appearances of Shakespeare specifically and poetry in general suggest hopefulness, the possibility of finding comfort in art, and the survival of the soul in *Mrs. Dalloway*. Clarissa quotes Shakespeare's plays many times throughout the day. When she shops for flowers at the beginning of the novel, she reads a few lines from a Shakespeare play, *Cymbeline*, in a book displayed in a shop window. The lines come from a funeral hymn in the play that suggests death should be embraced as a release from the constraints of life. Since Clarissa fears death for much of the novel, these lines suggest that an alternative, hopeful way of addressing the prospect of death exists. Clarissa also identifies with the title character in *Othello*, who loves his wife but kills her out of jealousy, then kills himself when he learns his jealousy was unwarranted. Clarissa shares with Othello the sense of having lost a love, especially when she thinks about Sally Seton. Before the war, Septimus appreciated Shakespeare as well, going so far as aspiring to be a poet. He no longer finds comfort in poetry after he returns.

The presence of an appreciation for poetry reveals much about Clarissa and Septimus, just as the absence of such appreciation reveals much about the characters who differ from them, such as Richard Dalloway and Lady Bruton. Richard finds Shakespeare's sonnets indecent, and he compares reading them to listening in at a keyhole. Not surprisingly, Richard himself has a difficult time voicing his emotions. Lady Bruton never reads poetry either, and her demeanor is so rigid and impersonal that she has a reputation of caring more for politics than for people. Traditional English society promotes a suppression of visible emotion, and since Shakespeare and poetry promote a discussion of feeling and emotion, they

MOTIFS

belong to sensitive people like Clarissa, who are in many ways antiestablishment.

TREES AND FLOWERS

Tree and flower images abound in *Mrs. Dalloway*. The color, variety, and beauty of flowers suggest feeling and emotion, and those characters who are comfortable with flowers, such as Clarissa, have distinctly different personalities than those characters who are not, such as Richard and Lady Bruton. The first time we see Clarissa, a deep thinker, she is on her way to the flower shop, where she will revel in the flowers she sees. Richard and Hugh, more emotionally repressed representatives of the English establishment, offer traditional roses and carnations to Clarissa and Lady Bruton, respectively. Richard handles the bouquet of roses awkwardly, like a weapon. Lady Bruton accepts the flowers with a "grim smile" and lays them stiffly by her plate, also unsure of how to handle them. When she eventually stuffs them into her dress, the femininity and grace of the gesture are rare and unexpected. Trees, with their extensive root systems, suggest the vast reach of the human soul, and Clarissa and Septimus, who both struggle to protect their souls, revere them. Clarissa believes souls survive in trees after death, and Septimus, who has turned his back on patriarchal society, feels that cutting down a tree is the equivalent of committing murder.

WAVES AND WATER

Waves and water regularly wash over events and thoughts in *Mrs. Dalloway* and nearly always suggest the possibility of extinction or death. While Clarissa mends her party dress, she thinks about the peaceful cycle of waves collecting and falling on a summer day, when the world itself seems to say "that is all." Time sometimes takes on waterlike qualities for Clarissa, such as when the chime from Big Ben "flood[s]" her room, marking another passing hour. Rezia, in a rare moment of happiness with Septimus after he has helped her construct a hat, lets her words trail off "like a contented tap left running." Even then, she knows that stream of contentedness will dry up eventually. The narrative structure of the novel itself also suggests fluidity. One character's thoughts appear, intensify, then fade into another's, much like waves that collect then fall.

Traditional English society itself is a kind of tide, pulling under those people not strong enough to stand on their own. Lady Bradshaw, for example, eventually succumbs to Sir William's bullying, overbearing presence. The narrator says "she had gone under," that her will became "water-logged" and eventually sank into his. Septimus is also sucked under society's pressures. Earlier in the day, before he kills himself, he looks out the window and sees everything as though it is underwater. Trees drag their branches through the air as though dragging them through water, the light outside is "watery gold," and his hand on the sofa reminds him of floating in seawater. While Septimus ultimately cannot accept or function in society, Clarissa manages to navigate it successfully. Peter sees Clarissa in a "silver-green mermaid's dress" at her party, "[l]olloping on the waves." Between her mermaid's dress and her ease in bobbing through her party guests, Clarissa succeeds in staying afloat. However, she identifies with Septimus's wish to fight the cycle and go under, even if she will not succumb to the temptation herself.

SYMBOLS

Symbols are objects, characters, figures, or colors used to represent abstract ideas or concepts.

THE PRIME MINISTER
The prime minister in *Mrs. Dalloway* embodies England's old values and hierarchical social system, which are in decline. When Peter Walsh wants to insult Clarissa and suggest she will sell out and become a society hostess, he says she will marry a prime minister. When Lady Bruton, a champion of English tradition, wants to compliment Hugh, she calls him "My Prime Minister." The prime minister is a figure from the old establishment, which Clarissa and Septimus are struggling against. *Mrs. Dalloway* takes place after World War I, a time when the English looked desperately for meaning in the old symbols but found the symbols hollow. When the conservative prime minister finally arrives at Clarissa's party, his appearance is unimpressive. The old pyramidal social system that benefited the very rich before the war is now decaying, and the symbols of its greatness have become pathetic.

PETER WALSH'S POCKETKNIFE AND OTHER WEAPONS
Peter Walsh plays constantly with his pocketknife, and the opening, closing, and fiddling with the knife suggest his flightiness and inability to make decisions. He cannot decide what he feels and doesn't know whether he abhors English tradition and wants to fight it, or whether he accepts English civilization just as it is. The pocketknife

reveals Peter's defensiveness. He is armed with the knife, in a sense, when he pays an unexpected visit to Clarissa, while she herself is armed with her sewing scissors. Their weapons make them equal competitors. Knives and weapons are also phallic symbols, hinting at sexuality and power. Peter cannot define his own identity, and his constant fidgeting with the knife suggests how uncomfortable he is with his masculinity. Characters fall into two groups: those who are armed and those who are not. Ellie Henderson, for example, is "weaponless," because she is poor and has not been trained for any career. Her ambiguous relationship with her friend Edith also puts her at a disadvantage in society, leaving her even less able to defend herself. Septimus, psychologically crippled by the literal weapons of war, commits suicide by impaling himself on a metal fence, showing the danger lurking behind man-made boundaries.

THE OLD WOMAN IN THE WINDOW

The old woman in the window across from Clarissa's house represents the privacy of the soul and the loneliness that goes with it, both of which will increase as Clarissa grows older. Clarissa sees the future in the old woman: She herself will grow old and become more and more alone, since that is the nature of life. As Clarissa grows older, she reflects more but communicates less. Instead, she keeps her feelings locked inside the private rooms of her own soul, just as the old woman rattles alone around the rooms of her house. Nevertheless, the old woman also represents serenity and the purity of the soul. Clarissa respects the woman's private reflections and thinks beauty lies in this act of preserving one's interior life and independence. Before Septimus jumps out the window, he sees an old man descending the staircase outside, and this old man is a parallel figure to the old woman. Though Clarissa and Septimus ultimately choose to preserve their private lives in opposite ways, their view of loneliness, privacy, and communication resonates within these similar images.

THE OLD WOMAN SINGING AN ANCIENT SONG

Opposite the Regent's Park Tube station, an old woman sings an ancient song that celebrates life, endurance, and continuity. She is oblivious to everyone around her as she sings, beyond caring what the world thinks. The narrator explains that no matter what happens in the world, the old woman will still be there, even in "ten million years," and that the song has soaked "through the knotted roots of infinite ages." Roots, intertwined and hidden beneath the earth, suggest the deepest parts of people's souls, and this woman's song touches everyone who hears it in some way. Peter hears the song first and compares the old woman to a rusty pump. He doesn't catch her triumphant message and feels only pity for her, giving her a coin before stepping into a taxi. Rezia, however, finds strength in the old woman's words, and the song makes her feel as though all will be okay in her life. Women in the novel, who have to view patriarchal English society from the outside, are generally more attuned to nature and the messages of voices outside the mainstream. Rezia, therefore, is able to see the old woman for the life force she is, instead of simply a nuisance or a tragic figure to be dealt with, ignored, or pitied.

SYMBOLS

Summary and Analysis

Part 1: From the opening scene, in which Clarissa sets out to buy flowers, to her return home. Early morning–11:00 a.m.

> *For Heaven only knows why one loves it so, how one sees it so, making it up, building it round one, tumbling it, creating it every moment afresh; but the veriest frumps, the most dejected of miseries sitting on doorsteps (drink their downfall) do the same; can't be dealt with, she felt positive, by Acts of Parliament for that very reason: they love life.*
>
> (See Quotations, p. 57)

Summary

Clarissa Dalloway, an upper-class, fifty-two-year-old woman married to a politician, decides to buy flowers herself for the party she is hosting that evening instead of sending a servant to buy them. London is bustling and full of noise this Wednesday, almost five years after Armistice Day. Big Ben strikes. The king and queen are at the palace. It is a fresh mid-June morning, and Clarissa recalls one girlhood summer on her father's estate, Bourton. She sees herself at eighteen, standing at the window, feeling as if something awful might happen. Despite the dangers, and despite having only a few twigs of knowledge passed on to her by her childhood governess, Clarissa loves life. Her one gift, she feels, is an ability to know people by instinct.

Clarissa next runs into her old friend Hugh Whitbread. Hugh and Clarissa exchange a few words about Hugh's wife, Evelyn, who suffers from an unspecified internal ailment. Beside the proper and admirable Hugh, Clarissa feels self-conscious about her hat.

Past and present continue to intermingle as she walks to the flower shop. She remembers how her old friend Peter Walsh disapproved of Hugh. She thinks affectionately of Peter, who once asked her to marry him. She refused. He made her cry when he said she would marry a prime minister and throw parties. Clarissa continues to feel the sting of his criticisms but now also feels anger that Peter did not accomplish any of his dreams.

She continues to walk and considers the idea of death. She believes she will survive in the perpetual motion of the modern London streets, in the lives of her friends and even strangers, in the trees, in her home. She reads lines about death from a book in a shop window. Clarissa reflects that she does not do things for themselves, but in order to affect other people's opinions of her. She imagines having her life to live over again. She regrets her face, beaked like a bird's, and her thin body. She stops to look at a Dutch picture, and feels invisible. She is conscious that the world sees her as her husband's wife, as Mrs. Richard Dalloway.

Clarissa looks in the window of a glove shop and contemplates her daughter, Elizabeth, who cares little for fashion and prefers to spend time with her dog or her history teacher, Miss Kilman, with whom she reads prayer books and attends communion. Clarissa wonders if Elizabeth is falling in love with Miss Kilman, but Richard believes it is just a phase. Clarissa thinks of her hatred for Miss Kilman, which she is aware is irrational, as a monster.

A car backfires while Clarissa is in the flower shop, and she and several others turn to observe the illustrious person passing in a grand car. They wonder if it is the queen or the prime minister behind the blinds. The car inspires feelings of patriotism in many onlookers.

Septimus Warren Smith, a veteran of World War I who is about thirty years old, also hears the car backfire. He suffers from shell shock, a mental illness brought on by the horrors of war, and believes he is responsible for the traffic congestion the passing car causes. Lucrezia, or Rezia, his young Italian wife, is embarrassed by his odd manner and also frightened, since Septimus recently threatened to kill himself. She leads him to Regent's Park, where they sit together. Septimus's thoughts are incomprehensible to his wife. He believes he is connected to trees and that trees must not be cut down. He believes that if he looks beyond the park railings he will see his dead friend, Evans, and fears the world might burst into flames. Septimus, Rezia, and many minor characters observe a plane overhead writing letters in the sky. The letters eventually seem to read "TOFFEE." Septimus believes someone is trying to communicate with him in a coded language. Rezia cannot stand to see him so broken, staring and talking out loud, and she walks to the fountain. She sees a statue of an Indian holding a cross. She feels alone and for a moment is angry with Septimus—after all, Dr. Holmes has said that Septimus has nothing at all the matter with him. Suddenly, Rezia feels her devotion to her husband clearly and returns to where he sits. A young woman, Maisie Johnson, asks them directions, and as she walks away she thinks about how strange the couple is. An older woman, Carrie Dempster, observes Maisie and feels regret about her own life.

ANALYSIS

Woolf wrote much of *Mrs. Dalloway* in free indirect discourse. We are generally immersed in the subjective mental world of various characters, although the book is written in the third person, referring to characters by proper names, as well as the pronouns *he*, *she*, and *they*. Woolf seldom uses quotation marks to indicate dialogue, as in most of Clarissa's encounter with Hugh Whitbread, to ensure that the divide between characters' interior and exterior selves remains fluid. In this way, Woolf allows us to evaluate characters from both external and internal perspectives: We follow them as they move physically through the world, all the while listening to their most private thoughts. The subjective nature of the narrative demonstrates the unreliability of memory. In this section, Clarissa, Septimus, and other characters interpret and reinterpret themselves and others constantly—changing their minds, misremembering, contradicting previous statements. Even simple facts, such as somebody's age, are occasionally vague, since people's memories are different and sometimes wrong.

Clarissa gains texture and depth as her thoughts dip frequently into the past and begin to edge around the future and her own mortality. Clarissa is full of happy thoughts as she sets off to buy flowers that beautiful June morning, but her rapture reminds her of a similar June morning thirty years earlier, when she stood at the window at Bourton and felt something awful might happen. Tragedy is never far from her thoughts, and from the first page of the book Clarissa has a sense of impending tragedy. Indeed, one of the central dilemmas Clarissa will face is her own mortality. Even as Clarissa rejoices in life, she struggles to deal with aging and death. She reads two lines about death from an open book in a shop window: "Fear no more the heat o' the sun / Nor the furious winter's rages." The words are from one of Shakespeare's later plays, *Cymbeline*, which is experimental and hard to classify, since it has comic, romantic, and tragic elements, much like *Mrs. Dalloway*. The lines are from a funeral song that suggests death is a comfort after life's hard struggles. Both Clarissa and Septimus repeat these lines throughout the day.

Though Septimus shares many of Clarissa's traits, he reacts differently to the passing car that thrills Clarissa and other bystanders. World War I has prompted changes in traditional English society, and many of London's inhabitants are lost in this more modern, more industrial society. People in the street, including Clarissa, seek meaning in the passing car, whose grandeur leads them to suspect it may carry the queen or a high-ranking government official. They want desperately to believe that meaning still exists in tradition and in the figureheads of England. For Septimus, the car on the street in the warm June sun does not inspire patriotism but rather seems to create a scene about to burst into flame. He has lost faith in the symbols Clarissa and others still cling to. The car's blinds are closed, and its passenger remains a mystery. Any meaning the crowd may impart on the car is their own invention—the symbol they want the car to be is hollow.

Woolf reveals mood and character through unusual and complex syntax. The rush and movement of London are reflected in galloping sentences that go on for line after line in a kind of ecstasy. These sentences also reflect Clarissa's character, particularly her ability to enjoy life, since they forge ahead quickly and bravely, much as Clarissa does. As Clarissa sees the summer air moving the leaves like waves, sentences become rhythmic, full of dashes and semicolons that imitate the choppy movement of water. Parentheses abound, indicating thoughts within thoughts, sometimes related to the topic at hand and sometimes not. Simple phrases often appear in the flow of poetic language like exclamations, such as when young Maisie Johnson encounters the strange-seeming Smiths and wants to cry "Horror! horror!" This line echoes Joseph Conrad's novel *Heart of Darkness*, in which a character despairs over humanity's cruelty. Later in the novel, we learn that Clarissa herself said "Oh this horror!" when Peter Walsh and Joseph Breitkopf, an old family friend, interrupted her encounter with Sally on the terrace. Society closes in on both Septimus and Clarissa, and the effect, conveyed through language and sentence structure, is terrible.

PART 2: FROM CLARISSA'S RETURN FROM THE SHOPS THROUGH PETER WALSH'S VISIT. 11:00 A.M.–11:30 A.M.

She had a perpetual sense, as she watched the taxi cabs, of being out, out, far out to sea and alone; she always had the feeling that it was very, very dangerous to live even one day.

(See QUOTATIONS, *p. 58)*

SUMMARY

Clarissa enters her home, feeling like a nun who has left the world and now returns to the familiar rituals of a convent. Although she does not believe in God, the moment is precious to her, like a bud on the tree of life. She is upset to learn that Richard has been invited to lunch at Lady Bruton's house without her. Ascending to her attic bedroom, Clarissa continues to reflect on her own mortality.

As Clarissa takes off her yellow-feathered hat, she feels an emptiness at the heart of her life. She has slept alone since she was ill with influenza but is happy to be solitary. She does not feel passionate about Richard and believes she has failed him in this regard. She feels sexual attraction to women and thinks she was in love with her friend Sally Seton, who spent a summer at Bourton.

Sally Seton, in Clarissa's memory, was a wild, cigarette-smoking, dark-haired rebel. Once Sally ran naked through the hallway at Bourton. Her behavior frequently shocked Clarissa's old Aunt Helena. Clarissa and Sally planned to change the world. Under Sally's influence, Clarissa began to read Plato in bed before breakfast and to read Shelley for hours. Clarissa remembers going downstairs in a white dress to meet Sally, thinking of a line from Shakespeare's play *Othello*—if it were now to die 'twere now to be most happy." Like Othello, she believes that if she were to die at that moment, she would be quite happy. Othello kills his wife, Desdemona, out of jealousy, then kills himself when he finds out his jealousy is unwarranted. The most exquisite moment of Clarissa's life occurred on the terrace at Bourton when, one evening, Sally picked a flower and kissed her on the lips. For Clarissa, the kiss was a religious experience. Peter Walsh interrupted the young women on the terrace, as thoughts of him now interrupt Clarissa's recollection of Sally. Clarissa always wanted Peter's good opinion, and she wonders what he will think of her now.

The house buzzes with pre-party activity, and Clarissa begins to mend the green dress she will wear that night. She shows an interest in her servants and is sensitive to their workload. She wants to be generous and is grateful to her servants for allowing her to be so. She sits quietly with her sewing, thinking of life as a wave that begins, collects, and falls, only to renew and begin again.

The front doorbell rings, and Peter Walsh surprises Clarissa with an unexpected visit. Peter plays with his pocketknife, as he always did, and feels irritated with Clarissa for the kind of life she's chosen to live with conservative Richard. Seeing that she's been mending a dress, he assumes she has simply been wasting time with parties and society since he left for India, shortly after Clarissa rejected his marriage proposal. He says he is in town to arrange a divorce for his young fiancée, Daisy, who lives in India and has two children. He imagines the Dalloways consider him a failure. Clarissa feels like a frivolous chatterbox around Peter. Moved by his memories and made sensitive by the sheer struggle of living, Peter bursts into tears. To comfort him, Clarissa takes his hand and kisses him. She wonders briefly to herself whether she would have been happier if she had married Peter instead of Richard. Peter asks Clarissa if she is happy, but Elizabeth enters the room before she can answer. As Peter leaves, Clarissa calls after him, "Remember my party to-night!"

ANALYSIS

Middle-aged Clarissa struggles to find her role in a society that places great importance on fulfilling sexual stereotypes. Clarissa feels invisible, virginal, and nunlike now that she is over fifty and will not have any more children. She feels silly in her yellow-feathered hat in front of Hugh, because Hugh is handsome and well dressed, and in some ways Clarissa now feels as if she has no sexuality. Clarissa's daughter, Elizabeth, is nearly grown, and now, with mothering behind her, Clarissa tries to discover her purpose in life, since women of her class and generation were not trained for careers. Clarissa feels her role is to be a meeting-point for others. She gathers people together, as she will at her party that night. No matter how uneasy she feels in her own life, she hides it so that others can feel comfortable. She sews the torn folds of her party dress back into place, masking both the flaws in the fabric and her own uneasiness. She even gathers herself together by pursing her lips and making her face into "one diamond." She feels it is her job to be a refuge for others and to conceal the strain and artificiality of gathering diverse parts of life together.

The difficulty of reconciling her innermost self with her exterior or surface self weighs constantly on Clarissa's mind, and the doors and windows that appear throughout the book represent this conflict symbolically. At Clarissa's house, workers take the doors off the hinges for the party, where Clarissa will gather people together and try to facilitate communication. She remembers that the blinds used to flap at Bourton, during a time when her need for privacy and her desire for communication were both, to some degree, attainable. Peter himself, in some ways, serves as a doorway between Clarissa's two selves. Through him, Clarissa can return to the days at Bourton and evaluate her choices, as though she can go back in time and change her mind. When Peter runs from the room and leaves her house, the noise from the open door is overwhelming and makes Clarissa's voice almost disappear. In his absence, real life, the present, sets in again. In real life, Clarissa is torn between the need for solitude and the glimmering surface world of society, and trying to move between the two states of being is almost a physical effort, much like physically removing doors from hinges.

Characters continually interrupt one another's significant moments of communication. Peter interrupts Clarissa's revelatory moment with Sally at Bourton, intervening before the women's intimacy can continue or intensify. Elizabeth interrupts Peter's encounter with Clarissa, another interruption that thwarts intimacy, stopping them from delving too deeply into their private feelings. Clarissa and Peter are both critical judges of others' characters, and they meet like challengers, Peter with his knife in his hand and Clarissa with her scissors. They are conscious of one another's failures—and of their own. This moment with Peter is charged with the potential to set Clarissa's life on a new course, whether Peter reveals lingering feelings or simply raises doubts in Clarissa's mind. For better or worse, Elizabeth halts the communication of their interior selves with her entry. Time moves on, and Peter walks out. Clarissa struggles to maintain communication and reminds him about her party, but her voice nearly disappears in the rush of the opening and closing door.

Clarissa is aware of having compromised by marrying Richard, who offered her a traditional, safe life path that is less threatening than the passion-filled path Peter or even Sally could have offered her. Though she enjoys beautiful things and society and appreciates the privacy she has with Richard, she is dissatisfied in some ways and worries that she fails to satisfy him as well. Richard, unlike more passionate characters, such as Sally and Septimus, has no association with nature, which underscores his pedestrian personality. Clarissa has found safety and comfort with Richard, a simple upholder of English tradition, but she felt passionate love for Sally, who subverted that tradition in many ways. Sally sold a family heirloom to go to Bourton, held feminist views, and shocked the upholders of old England, such as Aunt Helena. Clarissa describes her feeling for Sally as a match that burns in a crocus, a type of flower. The natural imagery of heat and flames often marks the thoughts of characters who feel deeply, including Clarissa and Septimus. The fire is spectacular, but never without threat. Richard is the foundation of her life, Clarissa admits, but part of her wonders what life could have been like without him, danger and all.

The line Clarissa quotes from *Othello* not only foreshadows Septimus's suicide but also points to the magnitude of Clarissa's own youthful feelings for Sally. In the play, Othello fervently loves his wife, Desdemona, but eventually kills her out of mistaken jealousy. Tortured by regret, Othello then kills himself. Othello cannot trust his good fortune, and loses it. By likening herself to Othello and Sally to Desdemona, Clarissa suggests not only the depth of her feeling, but also that it was she who killed the possibility of love with Sally—and with that some part of herself.

PART 3: FROM PETER LEAVING CLARISSA'S HOUSE THROUGH HIS MEMORY OF BEING REJECTED BY CLARISSA. 11:30 A.M.–11:45 A.M.

This late age of the world's experience had bred in them all, all men and women, a well of tears. Tears and sorrows; courage and endurance; a perfectly upright and stoical bearing.

(See QUOTATIONS, *p. 59)*

SUMMARY

We share Peter's point of view as he leaves Clarissa's house. Peter believes Clarissa has grown hard and sentimental. He criticizes her harshly to himself, thinking unhappily that her girlhood timidity has become conventionality in middle age. Then he begins to worry that he annoyed her with his unexpected visit and is embarrassed for having wept in her presence. One moment Peter feels thrilled that he is in love with Daisy and has a life in India about which Clarissa knows nothing, while the next moment he feels anew the blow of Clarissa having rejected him thirty years before. The sound of St. Margaret's bell sounding the half-hour makes him think of Clarissa's death, which upsets him, as does the thought of growing old himself.

Though he will eventually have to ask Richard's help in finding a job, Peter tells himself he does not care a straw what the Dalloways think of him. He admits he has been a failure in some sense, as when he was expelled from Oxford, but he feels the future lies in the hands of young men such as he was. A group of military boys march by, and Peter feels respect for them.

In the middle of Trafalgar Square, Peter feels suddenly free. Nobody except Clarissa knows he is in London. He begins to follow a young woman who seems to become his ideal woman as he looks at her. He compares her to Clarissa and decides that she is not rich or worldly, as Clarissa is. He wonders if she is respectable. Peter feels like a romantic buccaneer and is impressed by his own adventurousness. The woman takes out her keys and enters her house, never having spoken to Peter, which does not trouble him very much. He thinks of Clarissa telling him to remember her party that night.

Peter decides to sit in Regent's Park and smoke before his appointment with the lawyers, with whom he will arrange Daisy's divorce. He observes London and is proud of its level of civilization. He remembers how he was unable to get along with Clarissa's father. Having chosen a seat beside an elderly gray-haired nurse with a baby asleep in its stroller, Peter remembers Elizabeth. He expects that Elizabeth does not get along with Clarissa, as he feels Clarissa has a tendency to overdo things, which might embarrass Elizabeth. Soon Peter falls asleep.

He dreams about a solitary traveler who conceives of different images of women. The traveler, who seems to be Peter himself, imagines a woman made of sky and branches who bestows compassion and absolution. He imagines this woman as a siren, someone who might lure him to his death with her beauty. Finally, he imagines a mother figure who seems to wait for his return. When the image of the woman, now a landlady, asks if she can get the solitary traveler anything else at the end of the dream, he realizes he does not know to whom he can reply.

Peter wakes up saying "The death of the soul," and he links the dream and those words to a scene from Bourton in the early 1890s. That summer, Clarissa is shocked to hear about a neighbor who had a baby before she was married. Clarissa's prudish reaction makes Peter feel that the moment marks the death of her soul. Her reaction seemed not only prudish but also arrogant, judgmental, and unimaginative, and others who were at the table at the time were uncomfortable with her blatant scorn of and lack of sympathy for the woman.

Richard Dalloway comes to Bourton for dinner that night, and Peter knows immediately that Clarissa will marry Richard, toward whom she seems maternal. Peter finally decides to confront her about his own feelings. They meet by a broken fountain that dribbles water, and Peter demands the truth. Clarissa tells him it is no use, that she will not marry him. Peter leaves Bourton that night.

ANALYSIS

Peter Walsh is insecure and unsure about who he is, and these weaknesses in his character complicate his interactions with the world. Though likeable and fun to be around, Peter is highly critical of himself and others. He rarely voices these criticisms, but they echo constantly in his mind. The passage of time and the prospect of death frighten him, since he feels he has not accomplished anything substantial. He even goes out of his way to find a seat in the park where people are unlikely to ask him the time, since the question makes him nervous. Peter enjoys the sight of military boys passing by, because they seem oblivious to the reality of death and remind him of his own youth, when anything seemed possible. He takes an ironic pride in the civilization of London, with its butlers and chow dogs. He criticizes shallowness in others, particularly in Clarissa, but cannot help being attracted to a country that enjoys its excesses at the expense of colonies like India. England is broken, as Septimus's narrative makes clear, and any appearance of civilization does not go below the surface.

Peter frequently invents life to satisfy his own needs and desires and to make sense of the world. If we are bombarded with impressions, or atoms, as Woolf suggested, then a love of life involves giving shape to the multitude of impressions. Peter takes this idea of constructing reality to a new level when he follows the anonymous young woman in the street. Through this imaginary escapade, he successfully forgets about his own aging and temporarily escapes from his reality. In the constant motion of an urban setting like London, actual meaningful encounters with people are rare, and Peter invents both his interaction with this woman and its meaning. Peter later sees the Smiths. Even though he observes that they are in some kind of trouble, he does not talk to them. He prefers to exercise his control over a fantasy he knows will not be realized.

Peter wants to be saved, and he seeks redemption through relationships with women. He believes that women can offer him solace, much as religion comforts others, such as Miss Kilman. Immature even in his mid-fifties, he feels he has suffered a great deal and that his nature is particularly sensitive. Clarissa sensed Peter's huge, draining neediness in her youth, when she refused his marriage proposal. In the present, she wonders if life with Peter might have been more exciting than life with Richard, but at the same time she knows that Peter is too obsessed with himself to have been a good partner. In his dream Peter stereotypes women, imagining mother figures as well as cruel and beautiful temptresses. Peter is deluded in his wish to be saved by a female figure, and the traveler in the dream eventually realizes he has nobody to express his need to—there is no one for him to share his difficulties with. In the modern world, no God or woman or any figure at all exists to save him in the way he wishes to be saved.

Peter continues to seek Clarissa's approval and attention thirty years after she turned down his marriage proposal. Clarissa is the first person Peter goes to see upon his arrival in London, and he spends his entire day thinking about her and telling himself that he is no longer in love with her. He reminds himself that he no longer loves her so frequently that we seriously doubt the truth of his conviction. Clarissa has had as profound an effect on his life as he has had on hers. He still sees much of the world through her eyes, just as his criticisms still affect Clarissa's thoughts. Even his lover, Daisy, and her two children seem to improve when he observes them through Clarissa's gaze. Though outwardly self-assured, Peter is inwardly full of self-doubt and still needs Clarissa to bolster him up after all these years.

PART 4: FROM LITTLE ELISE MITCHELL RUNNING INTO REZIA'S LEGS TO THE SMITHS' ARRIVAL ON HARLEY STREET. 11:45 A.M.–12:00 P.M.

Clarissa had a theory in those days . . . that since our apparitions, the part of us which appears, are so momentary compared with the other, the unseen part of us, which spreads wide, the unseen might survive, be recovered somehow attached to this person or that, or even haunting certain places after death . . . perhaps— perhaps.

(See QUOTATIONS, *p. 60)*

SUMMARY

Peter watches a child in Regent's Park run into Rezia's legs. Rezia helps the child to stand up and thinks that she cannot tolerate Septimus's disturbing behavior anymore. Septimus says people are wicked. Once, by the river, he even suggested that he and Rezia kill themselves. He feels he knows the meaning of the world. A dog seems to become a man in front of his eyes. Rezia wishes she were back in Milan, making hats with her sisters. She tells Septimus it is time to go for his doctor's appointment. Septimus believes his dead friend, Evans, is walking toward them in the park, but the man approaching is actually Peter Walsh.

To Peter, the Smiths are simply a young couple having a lovers' quarrel. Peter marvels over the changes that have taken place in London since he was there five years ago, in 1918. Women are dressed well, and he likes their new habit of wearing makeup. He is impressed by the open-minded tone of newspapers and by the new sexually liberated generation.

Peter remembers Sally Seton flaring up at Hugh Whitbread in Bourton for his conservative views on women's rights. Sally told Hugh he represented all that was detestable about the British middle class. Peter loathes Hugh and his pretentiousness but also envies Hugh's success. He finds Richard Dalloway a dull but good man. Richard once said nobody should read Shakespeare's sonnets, because doing so was like listening at a keyhole.

Constantly returning to thoughts of Clarissa, Peter tells himself he is not in love with her anymore and reflects on her worldliness and her love of rank and tradition. Peter laments Clarissa's marriage, which forces her to quote Richard constantly, thus withholding her own thoughts. Peter feels that she has a genius for making her home a meeting place for young people and artists. He wonders if she gains insight from the philosophers she read as a girl, Huxley and Tyndall. When Clarissa was young, she saw a falling tree kill her sister, Sylvia. She did not become bitter, however, and continues to enjoy nearly everything.

Peter wonders if he is truly in love with Daisy, since he is not tortured over his relationship with her in the way he was with Clarissa. He is aware that he wants to marry her mainly because he doesn't want her to marry anyone else. Peter hears someone opposite the Regent's Park Tube station singing a song about love and death. The voice comes from a decrepit old woman, who at first seems sexless. She sings the line, "and if some one should see, what matter they?" Peter feels sorry for her and gives her a coin.

The point of view shifts to Rezia, who is also in the park. Initially, Rezia shares Peter's pity for the old woman, but the more Rezia listens, the more the song comforts her. She becomes hopeful that the psychiatrist Sir William Bradshaw will cure Septimus.

The point of view changes again, becoming closer to that of a traditional omniscient third-person narrator. We see Septimus and Rezia crossing the street and learn something of Septimus's past. Before the war, he was an aspiring poet and fell in love with Miss Isabel Pole, who gave lectures on Shakespeare. The point of view changes for a brief time to that of Mr. Brewer, Septimus's boss at the time at Sibleys and Arrowsmith, auctioneers, valuers, land and estate agents in London. Mr. Brewer thought Septimus had potential and, noticing that Septimus looked weak and unhealthy, recommended he play football. When Septimus went to fight in World War I, he became inseparable from his officer, Evans. Evans died, however, and Septimus felt nothing. Scared by his own lack of emotion, he married a young Italian woman, Lucrezia, when he was billeted in Milan.

Septimus begins to see ugliness in everything. Rezia wishes to have children, but Septimus does not want to bring children into the world or perpetuate the suffering he endures. His illness grows more severe, and Dr. Holmes comes to treat him. Holmes says Septimus is in a funk and that a trip to the music hall and a healthy diet should solve the problem. He feels the trouble is Septimus's nerves. Septimus sees Holmes as the embodiment of human nature, which has condemned him to death for his inability to feel. Finally, Holmes suggests that if the Smiths have no confidence in him, they should visit a specialist named Sir William Bradshaw.

ANALYSIS

Despite the disconnect between people in a modern urban setting like London, in this section we can see clearly the connection between Peter and Rezia. Woolf believed a complex web existed behind the "cotton wool" of the everyday, and this web allows her to make natural transitions between characters' points of view. Often a memory or a visual image links characters, and in this section several major links appear. One is the child Peter watches as it runs into Rezia's legs; another is the feeling of pity that an old woman singing in the street inspires in both Peter and Rezia. Parallels between Peter and Rezia allow us to compare as well as link them. Peter thinks of his rejection by Clarissa and cries that it was "awful, awful!" Several moments later, Rezia refers to Septimus's mental illness with precisely the same expression. Peter's self-pity at being spurned in love seems self-indulgent compared to the difficulties the Smiths must endure.

The old woman singing an ancient song is an affirming life force for Rezia. At first the woman seems sexless, and the song makes little sense. Both her physicality and her song become clearer under close observation. Though she is ancient, her song seems as though it will continue indefinitely, as will the love and death she sings of. Peter does not sense the joyfulness of this figure and feels only pity. Rezia, however, after her initial pity, draws strength from the woman and her words, "and if some one should see, what matter they?" Rezia is always very conscious of others' watchful eyes, such as those belonging to her neighbor Mrs. Filmer, but the song gives her renewed hope and faith in life. Rezia feels that outside observers keep her and Septimus continually under their judging gaze, and when she listens to the old woman she is able to step outside the judging gaze, if only for a moment.

Members of the upper class, such as Peter, Hugh, and Mr. Brewer, often turn a blind eye to the suffering of others. Though Peter criticizes Clarissa's worldliness, he is no better. He loves artifice and surfaces as much as anybody, admiring women's makeup and a military parade. When he passes by the distressed Smiths in the park, he knows Clarissa would likely have stopped to talk with them to find out what was wrong. Though Clarissa does not run bazaars or take an organized interest in the plight of the poor, she might have spoken to them because of her interest in the world, an interest that keeps her from becoming callow. Hugh Whitbread, on the other hand, never looks beyond the socks displayed in a department store window, and Septimus's boss, Mr. Brewer, resents the war mainly for what it did to his geranium beds. Though Clarissa is often as blind as anyone else, she is at least a close observer. She notices the world around her and wonders about the feelings of people beyond herself and her class.

PART 5: FROM SEPTIMUS'S APPOINTMENT WITH SIR WILLIAM BRADSHAW TO LUNCHTIME AT HALF-PAST ONE. 12:00 P.M.–1:30 P.M.

SUMMARY

As Big Ben strikes noon, Clarissa lays her green dress on her bed and the Smiths walk down Harley Street to Septimus's appointment with the celebrated psychiatrist Sir William Bradshaw. Known for his tact and understanding, Sir William is gray-haired and has an expensive gray car. He ascertains that Septimus is in a state of complete physical and nervous breakdown within two or three minutes of meeting him. When Sir William asks Septimus if he served with distinction in the war, Septimus thinks of the war as a "little shindy of schoolboys with gunpowder." Septimus tries to explain to the doctor that he has committed a terrible crime. Rezia protests that it is untrue, and the doctor takes her aside.

When Rezia admits that Septimus has threatened to commit suicide, Sir William prescribes a long period of bed rest in one of his homes in the country. Septimus will have to be separated from Rezia, though. Sir William prefers not to speak of "madness," but rather of a "lack of proportion." The son of a tradesman, Sir William never had time to read. He resents Septimus's shabbiness, as well as his cultivation.

Sir William tells Septimus that everybody has moments of depression and that nobody lives for himself alone. He reminds Septimus that he has a brilliant career ahead of him. Septimus feels he is being tortured by human nature in the form of Dr. Holmes and Sir William. He tries again to confess his crime, but he cannot remember what it is. He stammers out the pronoun *I*, and Sir William tells him not to think about himself. Sir William is eager to end the consultation and says he will let them know about the arrangements between five and six that evening. Rezia thinks Sir William has failed them and that he is not a nice man.

Sir William's philosophy of proportion involves prescribing weight gain and solitary rest. He secludes the mentally ill and forbids that they have children. His patients must conform to his sense of proportion, or he considers them mad. The narrator critiques Sir William's theories. Conversion, or pressure to conform to social norms, masquerades as brotherly love, but in colonies like India and at home in London, conversion is actually a quest for power. Sir William is in the business of colonizing people's minds. Lady Bradshaw lost touch with herself fifteen years ago, when her will succumbed to her husband's. Now she takes pictures of decaying churches and occupies herself with various causes.

Patients occasionally ask Sir William if the matter of living or not living is a personal choice. Though he shrugs his shoulders when asked if God exists, Sir William adamantly believes that no choice exists between life and death. He champions the prospects of brilliant careers, courage, and family affection. If a patient's "unsocial impulses" are out of control, he sends them away to a home. Sir William is greedy for dominion and impresses his will on the weak.

ANALYSIS

The link between Clarissa and Septimus intensifies with their respective actions at noon, a moment in which one character is very nearly the opposite of the other. Clarissa puts down her party dress, which is part of the front she puts on for society. Septimus, at the same time, is exposed to society as he enters Sir William Bradshaw's office for his appointment. Septimus sees doctors as the embodiment of human nature, which he saw at its ugliest during the war. Both Dr. Holmes and Sir William are older men who probably did not see any of the war firsthand, but they—and others—believe themselves to be experts on Septimus's condition. Clarissa, by mending and preparing the dress, will be able to navigate social situations smoothly. Septimus does not have, and does not want, Clarissa's charm and ability, and he is at the doctors' mercy.

Science has become a new religion of sorts and Sir William is referred to as a "priest of science," indicating the power he has over his patients. Just as religious believers often try to convert nonbelievers, Sir William seeks to convert the mentally ill to his sense of proportion. He preys on people like a vampire, sucking their souls out until they are his obedient followers. His wife, Lady Bradshaw, was one of his victims. Lady Bradshaw's hobby, taking pictures of decaying churches, represents the twentieth-century transition from faith in religion or God to faith in science or technology. When the ill consider that no god exists, they begin to wonder if their life and death are perhaps in their own hands, but Sir William insists that his style of life is in fact the only choice. Patients must convert to the world as Sir William conceives it or else be considered insane. This bullying technique suffocates patients like Septimus, who saw the horrifying results of blind conformity during the war.

The question of what the war was fought to preserve is never far from Septimus's thoughts, and he suffers from the lingering uncertainty. Peter Walsh and Clarissa might see English tradition as noble and worth fighting for, but Septimus, the veteran, does not read meaning in the symbols of England, at least not conventional meaning. The grand car at the opening of the novel does not give him shivers of excitement, the way it does for the other spectators, but seems only to point to his guilt for not being able to feel. Septimus no longer knows what the war was for. This doubt suggests that the very foundation of English society, an oppressive class system benefiting only a small margin of society, is problematic. Sir William, however, is uninterested in discussing Septimus's loss of faith in England and believes individuality is a sign of mental illness. He wants patients to convert, conform, and forget about themselves and any doubts they may have about the war or the empire.

In *Mrs. Dalloway*, Septimus, Clarissa, Peter, and Sally are all readers, while Sir William, Hugh Whitbread, Richard Dalloway, and Lady Bruton are all nonreaders. Whether a character reads or does not read is a fairly reliable indication of their values and priorities, and tensions often rise between the two groups. For example, Sir William, a nonreader, is hostile to those who do read, like Septimus. Sir William finds Septimus's bookishness nearly as repulsive as his shabby wardrobe. He sees a probing of the soul as a sign of illness, and later Clarissa, Peter, and Sally will share Septimus's instinctive dislike for him. An interest in words also relates to an interest in the soul. Readers, particularly Clarissa and Septimus, who enjoy Shakespeare are deeper characters who probe surfaces and look beyond a thing's given or expected meaning.

PART 6: FROM HUGH WHITBREAD EXAMINING SOCKS AND SHOES IN A SHOP WINDOW BEFORE LUNCHING WITH LADY BRUTON THROUGH CLARISSA RESTING ON THE SOFA AFTER RICHARD HAS LEFT FOR THE HOUSE OF COMMONS. 1:30 P.M.– 3:00 P.M.

SUMMARY

Hugh Whitbread examines the shoes and socks in a shop window on Oxford Street before he lunches at Lady Bruton's with Richard Dalloway. Hugh is not a deep person, but he is very courteous in an old-fashioned way and always brings Lady Bruton a bunch of carnations when he visits. Lady Bruton's assistant, Milly Brush, cannot stand Hugh, but he is oblivious to her distain.

Lady Bruton, at sixty-two, prefers Richard to Hugh, but she feels Hugh is kind. She does not see the point of "cutting people up," the way Clarissa does. Lady Bruton announces to her two guests that she wants their help but says they will discuss business after they eat. A magnificent lunch appears like magic, served by discreet white-capped maids. Nobody seems to have paid for the food and the table seems to have set itself.

Richard thinks Lady Bruton, the descendent of a great general, should have been a general herself. She has a reputation for talking like a man. Richard has great respect for her and enjoys the notion of a well-set-up woman from a great family. Lady Bruton is anxious to talk to the men about her business, but decides to wait until after they drink their coffee.

Lady Bruton asks after Clarissa, who thinks Lady Bruton does not like her. Hugh brags that he met Clarissa that morning. Lady Bruton tells them that Peter Walsh is in town. They all remember how passionately in love with Clarissa Peter once was, as well as how he went to India and made a mess of things. Richard decides to go home after lunch and tell Clarissa he loves her. Milly Brush watches Richard and feels she might once have fallen in love with him. Lady Bruton, Richard, and Hugh all like Peter but feel helping him is impossible because of his flawed character.

Emigration to Canada is Lady Bruton's cause. Her letter-writing skills are poor, and she is unable to write to the *Times* about the issue. She has invited Hugh and Richard to lunch so they can help her. She thinks Hugh knows how to write a letter that appeals to editors. Richard finds Hugh's letter to be nonsense, but Lady Bruton is thrilled with it. She stuffs Hugh's carnations into the front of her dress and calls him "[m]y Prime Minister." Richard plans to write a history of Lady Bruton's family, and she tells him the papers are all in order for when the time comes, by which she means when the Labour Party comes into power. Richard reminds Lady Bruton about Clarissa's party.

The men leave and Lady Bruton lies on the sofa. She remembers herself as a girl, riding on her pony in the country and roughhousing with her brothers. Hugh and Richard seem attached to her by a thread, which grows thinner as they move farther from her.

Hugh and Richard look lazily into an antique shop window. Hugh considers buying a Spanish necklace for his wife, Evelyn. Richard, looking at the things in the shop, is struck by the emptiness of life.

Richard starts home toward Clarissa and wants to bring her something. He decides to buy a vast bouquet of red and white roses. He feels his life and marriage to Clarissa are miracles after the war. Richard thinks about social reforms when he passes a woman stretched on the ground. She is free of all ties and laughs at the sight of him when he passes, holding his bouquet like a weapon. He considers the problem of the female vagrant. He feels Clarissa wants his support.

At home, Clarissa is irritated because her frumpy cousin, Ellie Henderson, is coming to the party and because Elizabeth is praying with Miss Kilman. Richard enters, but he is unable to tell Clarissa he loves her. They talk and he holds her hand. Richard leaves for a meeting and sets Clarissa up for a rest on the sofa. Clarissa feels unhappy because Peter and Richard criticize her for liking parties. She decides she throws parties simply because she loves life—her parties are an offering.

ANALYSIS

Members of the upper class in *Mrs. Dalloway*, including Hugh Whitbread and Lady Bruton, are devoted to preserving their traditions and justify their supremacy by defending one another's faults. Thus Hugh, a shallow glutton, is indulged and defended by Lady Bruton and Clarissa, among others. Likewise, money and a lordly demeanor shelter the psychiatrist Sir William from judgment. Lady

Bruton would like to make the problems of the British Empire, such as unemployment, disappear by exporting them—and English families—to Canada. She has "lost her sense of proportion" in her Canada obsession, but she is exempt from the evil forces of Sir William, whereas Septimus is not, in part because she belongs to Sir William's class. The upper class lives in an insular and make-believe world that is declining, but they do not intend to acknowledge this decline. The Conservative Party is about to lose power and be replaced by the Labour Party, at which point Richard will retire and write a book about the great war-waging family of Lady Bruton. While Hugh might be preoccupied with society and Sir William with amassing power and money, they are forgiven their sins due to their social status. Miss Kilman in her ugly mackintosh and Septimus in his shabby coat will not be forgiven their sins, because they are not armored with money or status. Nobody will empower them or defend their faults.

Women of all classes have little power in *Mrs. Dalloway*. Lady Bruton, though she seems displaced in the feminine sphere and exhibits general-like qualities, becomes as helpless as a child when she faces writing a letter to the newspaper. Normally proud and serious, she shows ridiculous gratitude when Hugh arranges her thoughts in the manner accepted by the male establishment. When Richard sees a vagrant woman lying on the street, he sees not a figure rejoicing in her freedom, but rather a poor woman and a social problem that the government must deal with. Outside the repressive confines of society, the vagrant woman becomes a positive life force, like the old woman Peter and Rezia hear singing the ancient song. Richard, however, sees her only as a woman who needs his help, and he views Clarissa in somewhat the same way. Richard is a kind but simple thinker, and he finds reassurance in believing that women need him.

The luncheon at Lady Bruton's effectively highlights the differences between the English establishment and Clarissa. Though Clarissa is a member of the upper class and can occasionally be a snob, she asks herself questions, judges herself, and tries to discover the truth about the world. No one at the luncheon puts forth a similar effort. Furthermore, none of the people at the luncheon have any rapport with or know how to handle flowers, which seem to stand in for beauty and emotion. The flowers Hugh and Richard choose, carnations and roses, are traditional. Richard carries his flowers like a weapon, while Lady Bruton first holds them awkwardly by her lace collar, then stuffs them down the front of her

dress. Clarissa is natural around flowers, and they constantly sur-
round her, suggesting her connection to nature and the deeper
reaches of the soul. Finally, Clarissa believes that she throws parties
to create but wonders to whom she gives her creation. This question
echoes Peter's dream, when the solitary traveler wonders to whom
he can reply when the landlady asks if he needs anything. In the
modern world, people are alone; they have no one to answer their
questions or to make offerings to. Clarissa is aware of this tragedy of
the modern era, while the insular characters representing the
English establishment are not.

PART 7: FROM ELIZABETH TELLING HER MOTHER SHE IS GOING SHOPPING WITH MISS KILMAN THROUGH ELIZABETH BOARDING AN OMNIBUS TO RETURN HOME TO HER MOTHER'S PARTY. 3:00 P.M.–LATE AFTERNOON

SUMMARY

Elizabeth enters the room where her mother rests, while Miss Kilman waits outside on the landing, wearing an unflattering mackintosh coat. She is poor and feels Clarissa is foolish and
condescending. Miss Kilman thinks she has been cheated out of happiness. She was a victim of anti-German discrimination during the war,
due to her German ancestry and to the sympathetic attitude she dis-
plays toward the Germans, and the school where she taught fired her.
She became religious two years and three months ago. Now she feels
she does not envy women like Clarissa but merely pities them.

When Clarissa gets up to greet Miss Kilman, Miss Kilman wishes
to fell her like a tree. She wants to make Clarissa cry. Clarissa is
shocked by the hateful look in Miss Kilman's eyes and feels Miss Kilman has stolen Elizabeth from her. After a moment, Miss Kilman's
threat seems to shrink for Clarissa, and Clarissa laughs and says good-
bye. She calls out to remember her party. When they are gone, Clarissa
thinks that love and religion are the cruelest things in the world.

Clarissa watches an old woman in the house opposite hers climb
the stairs and look out the window, unaware that anybody watches. Clarissa often watches her do this and feels it means something good, which
she thinks is the possibility of true privacy. She does not think Miss Kil-

man's religion or Peter Walsh's being in love solves the mystery of the human soul. She has her room and the old woman has hers.

Miss Kilman thinks Clarissa laughed at her for her ugliness. She struggles to control her desire to resemble Clarissa and prays to God. All she lives for, besides Elizabeth, is food, tea, and a hot-water bottle at night. Miss Kilman thinks it is unjust that she must suffer while Clarissa has no hardships.

At the Army and Navy Stores, Miss Kilman buys a petticoat. Elizabeth guides her around like an unwieldy battleship. They have tea and Miss Kilman eats greedily, feeling resentment when a child next to them eats a pink cake she had her eye on. Miss Kilman tells Elizabeth that all professions are open to women of her generation and makes her consider the plight of the poor. Elizabeth regrets that Clarissa and Miss Kilman do not get along, though she is aware that Clarissa makes an effort. When Clarissa offered Miss Kilman flowers sent from Bourton, Miss Kilman squashed them in a bunch. Miss Kilman's self pity becomes overwhelming, and Elizabeth longs to leave her. Miss Kilman is desperate to keep Elizabeth at the table with her, but eventually Elizabeth leaves. Miss Kilman goes to Westminster Abbey and prays.

Meanwhile, Elizabeth gets on an omnibus to the Strand and rides through a busy working-class neighborhood that her family never visits. People have begun to notice Elizabeth's beauty, and she is obliged to go to parties. She would rather be in the country with her father and the dogs. She considers what she might do for a career, such as become a doctor or a farmer or go into Parliament. She is lazy and feels these ideas are silly, so she will say nothing about it. Elizabeth knows Clarissa will want her at home, so she boards another bus and returns home.

SUMMARY & ANALYSIS

ANALYSIS

Miss Kilman bullies with her religion just as Sir William Bradshaw bullies with his science. The world has treated Miss Kilman badly because of her poverty, her ugliness, even her German name. She seeks revenge and wants to make Clarissa, who is likeable and attractive, unhappy the way she is. A falling tree killed Clarissa's sister, and Miss Kilman would like to "fell" Clarissa. Trees, with their extensive root systems, are like the soul, so this metaphor suggests that Miss Kilman is out to kill souls, just as Sir William is. Clarissa feels this murderous impulse masquerades as love and finds the deception horrifying, especially since she believes Elizabeth is vulnerable to it. Clarissa sees religious, scientific, and romantic belief as false justification for the flaws and weaknesses in people's characters, and she does not feel that these beliefs can explain the mystery of human beings' isolation in a world of activity. Clarissa believes that everyone is responsible for themselves and for others. As a born-again Christian, Miss Kilman seeks to convert Elizabeth to her beliefs the way Sir William seeks to convert people to his idea of sanity. Because Miss Kilman is a woman, she does not have the opportunities for success as Sir William, but both characters thirst after domination in similar ways.

Elizabeth does not return Miss Kilman's lesbian attraction, as Clarissa suspected, but she is attracted to the new ideas and options that Miss Kilman puts before her, even if her laziness precludes her from pursuing them. Elizabeth enjoys exploring London for an afternoon and considers career options, but she is not a complex thinker like Clarissa. Though new careers are now open to women, Elizabeth is too passive to delve deeply into new territory. Richard says that if he had had a boy, he would have encouraged him to work, but he does not encourage Elizabeth in this regard. While the social climate is changing for women, it does not seem as though Elizabeth will take a groundbreaking path; it seems likely that she will probably follow her parents into an upper-class life.

The old woman Clarissa watches in the window reveals the human conflict at the heart of the novel—the interplay between communication and privacy. Clarissa struggles to understand why people need privacy, if they need it at all, and what makes communication so difficult. Clarissa and the old woman have been neighbors for years, but, though Clarissa knows the woman's movements, she does not know the woman's name. The woman is a mystery, and her distance is both a comfort and an ache for Clarissa. The human soul must exist alone and look to itself for answers, but it also craves communication and the company of others. The rooms of a house are a metaphor for the soul, a safe but empty place where one can hide from or ignore the judgmental eyes of the world. Like the house metaphor, the figure of the old woman also suggests both the solace of the human soul and its loneliness. The soul can be shared with others only to a small degree, though Clarissa tries to solve this dilemma by throwing parties and constantly calling out to people to remember them. Clarissa's reaching out is also limited, and no one even considers that Clarissa will invite Miss Kilman to the party that evening. Before Septimus's suicide, he sees an old man on the staircase opposite his window, a scene that parallels Clarissa's watching the old woman and emphasizes the extreme loneliness of characters living in their own private rooms.

PART 8: FROM SEPTIMUS OBSERVING DANCING SUNLIGHT IN HIS HOME WHILE REZIA WORKS ON A HAT THROUGH SEPTIMUS'S SUICIDE. LATE AFTERNOON—6:00 P.M.

SUMMARY

Septimus watches sunlight play on the wallpaper from the couch. He thinks of the line from the Shakespeare play *Cymbeline*: "Fear no more." Rezia sees him smile but is disturbed. Often he speaks nonsense or has visions, believing himself drowned or falling into flames. She feels that they no longer have a marriage.

Rezia makes a hat for Mrs. Peters, the married daughter of their neighbor Mrs. Filmer. Rezia talks, and Septimus begins to look around him. He says the hat is too small for Mrs. Peters and speaks in a lucid way for the first time in weeks. He and Rezia joke together, and Rezia is relieved that they're acting like a married couple. Septimus, who has a good eye for color, begins designing the hat. When he is finished, Rezia stitches it together. Septimus feels he is in a warm place, such as on the edge of the woods. He is proud of his work on Mrs. Peters' hat. In the future, Rezia will always like that hat, which they made when Septimus was himself.

Rezia worries when she hears a tap at the door. She thinks it might be Sir William, but it is only the young girl who brings them the evening paper. Rezia kisses the child, gets out a bag of sweets, and dances around the room with her. Rezia builds the moment up until it is something wonderful. Septimus reads the paper and grows tired. He feels happy. As he begins to fall asleep, the laughing voices begin to sound like cries.

Septimus wakes up terrified. Rezia has gone to bring the child back to her mother. Septimus feels he is doomed to be alone. Around him he sees only ordinary objects, like the coal-shuttle and bananas on the sideboard; he no longer sees the beauty of the afternoon. He calls out for Evans but receives no answer. Rezia returns and begins making an adjustment to Mrs. Peters' hat. Rezia feels she can now speak openly with Septimus. She remembers the first time she saw him, when he looked like a young hawk.

The time for Sir William's message to arrive is nearing. Septimus asks why Sir William has the right to tell him what he "must" do. Rezia says it is because he threatened to kill himself. Septimus asks for the papers on which he and Rezia wrote down his theories about beauty and death and tells Rezia to burn them all. However, Rezia thinks some of what he wrote is very beautiful, and she ties the papers in a piece of silk and puts them away. Rezia says she will go wherever Septimus goes. Septimus thinks she is a flowering tree and that she fears no one. He thinks she is a miracle.

Rezia goes to pack their things. She hears voices downstairs and worries that Dr. Holmes is calling. She runs down to prevent the doctor from coming upstairs. Septimus quickly considers killing himself by various methods and decides he must throw himself from the window. He does not want to die and thinks this is the doctors' idea of tragedy, not his or Rezia's; he thinks, "Life was good." An old man on a staircase across the way stares at him. Septimus hears Holmes at the door. He cries, "I'll give it you!" and flings himself out the window onto Mrs. Filmer's railings.

Holmes sees what Septimus has done and calls him a coward. Rezia understands what Septimus has done. Holmes gives her a glass of sweet liquid that makes her sleepy. Holmes does not think Rezia should see Septimus when paramedics carry him away, since his body is so mangled. Before falling asleep, Rezia sees the outline of Holmes's body against the window. She thinks, "So that was Dr. Holmes."

ANALYSIS

In this section, Septimus seems to come out of his illness into a kind of remission. He is lucid, sees the world through clear eyes, and does not hear voices. He watches Rezia playing with the child, building up the moment into something wonderful, the way Clarissa does when she walks through the London streets or throws a party. Clarissa and Rezia act as life forces in the novel, and both are compared to trees. Septimus feels he is on the edge of a forest, because his and Rezia's souls are now easy together, and they communicate naturally, like any other married couple, over the design of Mrs. Peters' hat. As Rezia sews, the pair converses intimately, the threads of their thoughts intermingling in a beautiful pattern. Septimus seems to forget the approach of the doctors. When he wakes up after helping

Rezia with the hat-making and sees he is alone, he experiences the same emotional shock as Clarissa did when she put down her yellow-feathered hat that morning and felt an emptiness at the heart of life. The world is beautiful, but Septimus's soul has been severely damaged by the war, and the beauty he sees is ephemeral. He tries to preserve this soul from the clutches of the overbearing doctors by asking Rezia to burn the papers on which he drew and wrote his thoughts over the period of his illness. Septimus's temporary sanity ends with his suicide.

Dr. Holmes's arrival forces Septimus to choose between committing suicide or surrendering his soul. Opting for death of the body instead of death of the soul, Septimus flings himself onto the railings beneath his window. Throughout the novel, houses and rooms serve as metaphors for the soul and its yearnings for privacy, and railings mark the border between the interior of the home and the public world of society. By throwing himself onto the railings, Septimus seems to attempt a kind of communication, while at the same time protecting his private soul from Holmes and Sir William. Before his plunge, Septimus sees an old man descending the staircase opposite his window. Unlike the old woman Clarissa observes ascending the staircase or wandering safely through the rooms of her home, the old man is symbolically leaving the privacy of his home. If Septimus must part with the privacy of his soul, he will make his soul public but refrain from sacrificing it. He does not want to die, but since he feels he has no alternative due to the doctors' threats, he will make the decision and perform the action himself. He demonstrates his refusal to let the doctors take his soul when he announces, "I give it you!" Nobody has taken Septimus's soul. The first-person pronoun indicates that he has given it himself. Though his death is tragic, he has maintained agency and dignity in choosing his destiny.

Septimus's suicide reveals the blindness of human nature as embodied by Holmes and Sir William. Before this point, Septimus had given many indications that he contemplated killing himself, the most obvious being when he openly says that it is his intention to do so. Yet Holmes, referring to the suicide, asks how it was possible to predict it would happen and decides that it was an impulsive act for which no one is to blame. These are absurd claims and questions, and they reveal Holmes's willful blindness to the truth. Nobody wishes to take responsibility for Septimus's death or to believe its cause to be anything beyond a spontaneous impulse. Holmes would rather the world sleep quietly and drugged, as he forces Rezia to do,

SUMMARY & ANALYSIS

rather than wake up and ask questions about human cruelty. Acknowledging Septimus's motivations would threaten the beliefs that are the foundation of the doctors' lives.

PART 9: FROM PETER WALSH HEARING THE SOUND OF AN AMBULANCE SIREN TO HIS OPENING HIS KNIFE BEFORE ENTERING CLARISSA'S PARTY. 6:00 P.M.–EARLY NIGHT

SUMMARY

Standing across from the British Museum, Peter Walsh hears the ambulance rush to pick up Septimus's body. He views the ambulance as one of the triumphs of civilization. The English health system strikes him as humane, and London's community spirit impresses him. As he walks toward his hotel, he thinks of Clarissa. They used to explore London together by riding the omnibus. Clarissa had a theory that to know somebody, one had to seek out the people and places that completed that person. She felt that people spread far beyond their own selves and might even survive in this way after death. Clarissa has influenced Peter more than anybody else he knows.

Peter arrives at his hotel and thinks about Clarissa at Bourton. They used to walk in the woods, argue, and discuss poetry, people, and politics. Clarissa was a radical in those days. At the hotel Peter receives a letter from Clarissa that says it was heavenly to see him that morning. He is upset by the letter, which seems like a "nudge in the ribs" after his vivid memories of Clarissa. The hotel now strikes Peter as frigid and impersonal. He imagines Clarissa regretting her refusal of his marriage proposal and then feeling sorry for him. He pictures her weeping as she wrote him the note.

Peter looks at a snapshot of Daisy with a fox terrier on her knee. She is dark and very pretty. Peter shaves and dresses for dinner. He wonders whether his marriage to Daisy would be good for her, as it would mean giving up her children and being judged by society. He is conflicted about Daisy. He does not like the idea of being faithful to her, but he hates the idea of Daisy being with anyone else. He quickly disregards the age difference between them and takes comfort in knowing she adores him. He decides that if he retires, he will write books.

At dinner, the other hotel guests find him appealing. His self-composure and serious approach to eating his dinner win him their respect. They like the way he orders Bartlett pears firmly. The guests wish to talk with one another, but they feel shy. In the smoking room, Peter and the Morris family make small talk. Peter thinks they like him. He decides to go to Clarissa's party to find out what the Conservatives are doing in India and to hear the gossip.

Peter sits in a wicker chair on the hotel steps. The night is hot but lighter than he is used to, because daylight savings has been introduced since he was last in London. He reads the paper and watches young people pass by on their way to the movies. He thinks the social structure is changing and that experience enriches life. He sets off for Clarissa's and feels that he is about to have an experience. He looks in people's lighted windows on his way and enjoys the richness of life. At Clarissa's house, Peter steels himself, opens the blade of his pocketknife, and enters the party.

ANALYSIS

The ambulance Peter hears is the one carrying Septimus's body, and Peter's adoring interpretation of the ambulance siren as a "triumph of civilization" is ironic, because Septimus has sought death to escape the very civilization Peter reveres. In the wailing siren, Peter hears all that is good about English society—its humanity, efficiency, and compassion. However, Septimus found those same things constricting and deadening, not liberating and inspiring. Peter stands across from the British Museum, a structure that suggests England's might, tradition, and imperial power. Septimus fought to preserve these virtues during the war, and they eventually became hollow and meaningless to him. Peter hears humanity in the ambulance siren, but the *in*humanity of the English medical system played a part in Septimus's death. Peter constantly notices the civilization of England, and the repetition of the word, juxtaposed with Septimus's death, calls Peter's accuracy into question. London is surely no gentler than the countries, such as India, England sets out to "civilize" through colonization. Likewise, the communal spirit Peter observes in London is also questionable, since the Londoners in the novel, even Peter himself, are incredibly isolated. Peter reads the world only superficially, seeing what he wants to see and not probing too deeply beneath the surface. Septimus perhaps probes too deeply, and he cannot bear what he finds. Both Septimus and Peter read the same cricket scores and the same news in the evening paper, a similarity that emphasizes the different ways in which each man interprets the same world.

Though Peter constantly doubts himself and his decisions, at the hotel and the dinner he momentarily reveals the kind of man he could be, or wants to be. Until now, Peter has seemed hysterical, bursting into tears in front of Clarissa and claiming madly to himself that he no longer loves her. At the hotel, however, he seems composed and in control. As he moves about his room, he imagines how Daisy sees him: as a reliable man who shaves, dresses, and takes firm control of life's small details. He suspects he cannot actually make her happy, and that she will be better off without him, but he seems to like the feeling of being depended on and looked up to by this younger, foolish girl. At the dinner Peter slides more fully into this version of himself. With dignified detachment he selects wine and eats his dinner, showing more composure than at any other point in the novel. When Peter orders his Bartlett pears, the new Peter seems to crystallize. He knows exactly what he wants, and says so clearly. Gone, for the moment, are the usual hemming and hawing, the incessant justifications and qualifications that usually bloat his thoughts and desires. For this short moment at the table he is comfortable in his own skin.

Clarissa recognizes the conflict between nurturing her need for privacy and fulfilling her desire to emerge and communicate with others, which is why she throws her parties. Peter compares people to fish that swim for ages in the gloomy depths and occasionally need to come to the surface and frolic in the "wind-wrinkled waves." People need to form community, however brief; they need to gossip at parties. The effort to communicate requires endurance, which is why Peter prepares himself and opens his knife before entering the party and why Clarissa purses her lips and creates a composed "diamond" face for the world. Septimus was tortured in the private world of his own soul after the war and, with his inability to hold himself together, was also at the mercy of the public world. He could no longer summon the endurance necessary to face the world or even exist in it, and even Peter and Clarissa hang on by only a thread— the tenuousness of which is emphasized by the knife and scissors with which they greet each other earlier in the day. Though Peter often misjudges and criticizes Clarissa, he admires her endurance and strength. Clarissa may have her failings and weaknesses, but her determination to stitch together her internal and external worlds, however briefly or infrequently, makes her a remarkable woman.

PART 10: FROM SERVANTS MAKING LAST-MINUTE PARTY PREPARATIONS THROUGH THE END OF THE PARTY AND THE APPEARANCE OF CLARISSA. EARLY NIGHT–3:00 A.M.

She felt somehow very like him—the young man who had killed himself. She felt glad that he had done it; thrown it away. The clock was striking. The leaden circles dissolved in the air. He made her feel the beauty; made her feel the fun. But she must go back. She must assemble.

(See QUOTATIONS, *p. 61*)

SUMMARY

The Dalloway servants rush around and make last-minute party preparations. The prime minister is supposed to arrive, but this does not make any difference to the cook, Mrs. Walker, who is overwhelmed with work. Dinner over, the female guests go upstairs and the men call to the kitchen for the Imperial Tokay, a sweet wine. Elizabeth worries about her dog and tells a servant to check on it.

More people arrive and the men join the women upstairs. Clarissa says, "How delightful to see you!" to everybody, which Peter finds insincere. He wishes he had stayed at home. Clarissa fears her party will be a failure. She is aware of Peter's critical eye but thinks she would rather be drenched in fire while attempting her party than fade like her meek cousin, Ellie Henderson.

The wind blows a curtain, and Clarissa sees a guest beat it back and go on talking. She thinks her party may be a success after all. Guests continue to arrive, but Clarissa does not enjoy herself. She feels anyone could take her role as hostess but is also somewhat proud of her party's success. The hired butler, Mr. Wilkins, announces Lady Rosseter, who turns out to be Sally Seton, now married. Sally heard about the party through a mutual friend and has arrived unexpectedly. Clarissa remembers the moment in her youth when she was thrilled merely to think of being under the same roof with Sally. She thinks Sally has lost her luster, but they laugh and embrace and seem ecstatic to see one another. With her old bravado and egotism, Sally says she has "five enormous boys."

The prime minister arrives, interrupting Clarissa's reunion with Sally. He does his rounds and retires to a little room with Lady Bruton. Peter Walsh catches sight of Hugh Whitbread and criticizes him mercilessly in his thoughts. Meanwhile, he watches Clarissa in her "silver-green mermaid's dress" and feels she still has the power to sum up all of life in a moment, merely by passing by and catching her scarf in some woman's dress. Peter reminds himself that he is not in love with her anymore.

Clarissa sees the prime minister off and thinks she does not feel passionate about seeing anyone. She prefers the intense hatred inspired by Miss Kilman, since the emotion is heartfelt. She returns to the party and mingles with her guests, all of whom seem to have failed in their lives in some regard. Mrs. Hilbery tells Clarissa she looks like her mother, and Clarissa is moved. Old Aunt Helena arrives and talks about orchids and Burma. Sally catches Clarissa by the arm, but Clarissa is busy and says she will come back later, meaning that she will talk to her old friends when the others have gone. Everyone's thoughts dip constantly into the past.

Clarissa must speak to the Bradshaws. She dislikes Sir William but tolerates Lady Bradshaw, who tells Clarissa about Septimus's suicide. Clarissa goes into the little room where the prime minister sat so she can be alone. She feels angry that the Bradshaws brought death to her party. She ruminates about Septimus's death and thinks he has preserved something that is obscured in her own life. She sees his death as an attempt at communication. She remembers the moment she felt she could die at Bourton in total happiness. She considers the young man's death her own disgrace.

Clarissa looks out the window and sees the old woman in the house across the way going to bed. She hears the party behind her and thinks of the words from Shakespeare's play *Cymbeline*: "Fear no more the heat of the sun." She identifies with Septimus and feels glad he has thrown his life away. She returns to the party, where Peter and Sally are gossiping about the past and present and wondering where she is. Sally goes to say goodnight to Richard. Peter is filled with terror and ecstasy when Clarissa appears.

ANALYSIS

Septimus's death makes Clarissa's party seem even more indulgent than it is. Elizabeth's obsession with her dog, the men's enjoyment of their wine, and Clarissa's gushing welcomes to guests all seem trivial in light of Septimus's suicide. More troubling is the fact that Clar-

issa's party entertains Septimus's oppressors, the upholders of sti-
fling British society, including Sir William. Most of the guests seem
to have failed in some way, and nearly all live in the bubble world of
upper-class England. Clarissa's stuffy Aunt Helena, the botanist
who believes in suppressing emotion and any interesting topic of
conversation, spent a lifetime weighing flowers down with books to
make them flat. This hobby suggests her wish to squash the human
soul in order to preserve the social mores of English society; it also
demonstrates the danger of applying analytic, scientific study to aes-
thetic values. The prime minister himself is present, a comical,
slightly pathetic figure who struggles to be a figurehead to a public
desperate for symbols. The social system is empty and even ridiculous, but Clarissa and her guests uphold it nonetheless.

Clarissa worries that the party will be a failure until she sees a
guest beat back a blowing curtain, which serves as a kind of border
between the private soul and the public world. Her guest refuses to
let the curtain get in the way of his talking, and his beating it back
reveals his dedication to communication. Clarissa imagined her
party as a forum for discussion of topics that people would not normally discuss, and people are indeed emerging somewhat from their
usual selves. The party seems to be a success. One of Clarissa's hap-
piest memories is of the blinds blowing at Bourton when she and her
friends were young and honest communication was possible to a
greater degree. As the old woman in the window across from Clarissa's window suggests, true communication becomes harder as one
grows older and more isolated. Clarissa's party provides an outlet,
however brief, where communication might take place once again.

Here at the party, for the first time, we see Sally Seton as she is in
the present, outside of Clarissa's memory. She swoops in unexpectedly, having heard of the party from a friend as she was passing
through town. Clarissa's first thought is that Sally looks nothing like
what she remembered—the luster has left her. She observes this
without judgment or reproach and still asserts that it is wonderful to
see her, but even then she adds that Sally is "less lovely." Clarissa
remembers with some disbelief the Sally from Bourton and cannot
reconcile those images with the Sally that has appeared in her home.
Brazen, wonderful, creative Sally is now the wife of a miner, the
mother of five sons, a gardener, and a lady (her married name is
Lady Rosseter). Though Clarissa loves flowers, she does not grow
them, and Sally's passion for her garden gives her an earthy and
immediate physicality that Clarissa lacks. Though Sally and Clar-

issa hug and kiss hello, this Sally seems less real than the Sally who has lurked in Clarissa's imagination all these years.

Sally's appearance at the party brings the past crashing into the present, and Clarissa, faced now with the real woman from her memories, must confront the present head-on. Clarissa and Sally barely have time to catch up before Clarissa leaves her with Peter to devote herself to other guests. Clarissa has spent years remembering, even lusting after, Sally, and now that Sally is here, in the flesh, Clarissa cannot face her; as with Peter and the young woman he follows, Clarissa prefers fantasy to reality. In many ways, Clarissa has spent her life stuck in Bourton, with her memories of Sally and her occasional regrets about Peter simmering constantly under the surface of her life. Now, here they are, the both of them—Sally and Peter—and Clarissa barely speaks to them. The feelings she has about them are distant and hollow, not within her heart but outside it. When she sees Peter and Sally talking and laughing about the past, she cannot join them. Only after watching the old woman next door and thinking about Septimus does she gather the courage to find them. To face the present fully she must first come to terms with her own aging and eventual death.

When Clarissa retreats to the small solitary room to reflect on Septimus's suicide, she experiences a powerful revelation, which is the climax of the novel. The impression of the prime minister's body is still on the chair in the room, emphasizing that the soul is never completely alone or free from the influence of social pressures. Clarissa feels that Septimus's death is her own disgrace, and she is ashamed that she is an upper-class society wife who has schemed and desired social success. His death is also her disgrace because she compromised her passion and her soul when she married Richard, while Septimus preserved his soul by choosing death. She remembers the line from Shakespeare's *Othello*, "If it were now to die, 'twere now to be most happy." She has lived to regret her decisions, just as Othello did. Clarissa sees her life clearly and comes to terms with her own aging and death, which ultimately enables her to endure. When she returns to the party, we see her from Peter's perspective, not her own, and the novel ends without any more glimpses into her mind.

IMPORTANT QUOTATIONS EXPLAINED

1. For Heaven only knows why one loves it so, how one sees it
so, making it up, building it round one, tumbling it, creating
it every moment afresh; but the veriest frumps, the most
dejected of miseries sitting on doorsteps (drink their
downfall) do the same; can't be dealt with, she felt positive,
by Acts of Parliament for that very reason: they love life.

This quotation, part of Clarissa's thoughts as she walks to the flower
shop in the early morning and Big Ben chimes the hour, reveals her
strong attachment to life and the concept of life as her own invention. The long, galloping sentence, full of commas and semicolons,
mirrors her excitement at being alive on this June day. Clarissa is
conscious that the impressions of the things around her do not nec-
essarily hold beauty or meaning in themselves, but that humans act
as architects, building the impressions into comprehensible and
beautiful moments. She herself revels in this act, in the effort life
requires, and she knows that even the most impoverished person living on the streets can derive the same wonder from living. She sees
that happiness does not belong to a particular class, but to all who
can build up a moment and see beauty around them. Later her husband Richard sees a vagrant woman on the street but classifies her
only as a social problem that the government must deal with. Clarissa believes that every class of people has the ability to conceptual-
ize beauty and enjoy life, and she therefore feels that government
intervention has limited uses. She does not equate class with happiness.

2.   She had a perpetual sense, as she watched the taxi cabs, of
      being out, out, far out to sea and alone; she always had the
      feeling that it was very, very dangerous to live even one day.

This quotation, which occurs during Clarissa's shopping expedition
when she pauses for a moment to look at the omnibuses in Piccadilly, emphasizes the contrast between the busyness of public life
and the quiet privacy of the soul. Clarissa, even when she is walking
in the crowded city streets, contemplates the essential loneliness of
life. The image of water acts much like the image of the sun in the
novel. The sun beats down constantly, sometimes creating a wonderful feeling of warmth, sometimes scorching unbearably. The
rhythmic movement of the sea's waves is similar. Sometimes the
cyclical movement is breathtaking, while sometimes it threatens to
drown whoever is too weak to endure the pressure, such as Lady
Bradshaw or Septimus. Each person faces these same elements,
which seems to join humans in their struggle. However, everyone is
ultimately alone in the sea of life and must try to stay afloat the best
they can. Despite the perpetual movement and activity of a large city
like London, loneliness is everywhere.

Clarissa's reflection occurs directly after she considers her old
friend Peter, who has failed to fulfill the dreams of his youth. As
Clarissa ages, she finds it more difficult to know anybody, which
makes her feel solitary. She hesitates to define even herself. Failing,
becoming overwhelmed by the pressures of life, and drowning are
far too easy. Clarissa is fifty-two, she's lived through a war, and her
experiences amplify the dangers of living and of facing the world
and other people.

3.   This late age of the world's experience had bred in them all, all men and women, a well of tears. Tears and sorrows; courage and endurance; a perfectly upright and stoical bearing.

This quotation occurs directly after Clarissa reads lines from Shakespeare's play *Cymbeline* in a bookshop window. The lines "Fear no more the heat o' the sun / Nor the furious winter's rages" come from a hymn sung at a funeral and suggest that death is a release from the hard struggle of life. The words speak very directly to Clarissa's own time period, the years after World War I. England is still in shock after having lost so many men in battle, the world now seems like a hostile place, and death seems like a welcome relief. After Clarissa reads the words from *Cymbeline*, she considers the great amount of sorrow every person now bears. Everyone, regardless of class, has to some degree been affected by the war.

Despite the upright and courageous attitudes many people maintain, they all carry a great sadness, and people cry constantly in *Mrs. Dalloway*. Peter Walsh bursts into tears at Clarissa's house. Clarissa's eyes fill with tears when she thinks of her mother walking in a garden. Septimus cries, and so does Rezia. Tears are never far from the surface, and sadness lurks beneath the busy activity of the day. Most people manage to contain their tears, according to the rules of society, or cry only in private. Septimus, the veteran, is the only character who does not hesitate to cry openly in the park, and he is considered mentally unstable. People are supposed to organize bazaars to help raise money for the veterans. People are supposed to maintain a stiff upper lip and carry on. Admitting to the horrors of the war by crying is not acceptable in English culture, though as Clarissa points out, a well of tears exists in each of them.

4.   Clarissa had a theory in those days . . . that since our
      apparitions, the part of us which appears, are so momentary
      compared with the other, the unseen part of us, which
      spreads wide, the unseen might survive, be recovered
      somehow attached to this person or that, or even haunting
      certain places after death . . . perhaps—perhaps.

This quotation occurs as Peter Walsh walks back to his hotel. He
hears the ambulance go by to pick up Septimus's body and remembers Clarissa's passion during their youth. Clarissa was frustrated at
how little one person could know another person, because she felt
that so much of a person existed out of reach of others. A person's
soul was like a plant or a tree, with a small part showing above-
ground and a complex, unseen root system existing underneath.
Although Clarissa had experienced death at a young age when her
sister Sylvia died, she did not want to believe that death was the
absolute end. Instead she believed that people survived, both in
other people and in the natural world. To know someone beyond
the surface, one had to seek out the people and places that completed that person. The structure of *Mrs. Dalloway* supports Clarissa's theory, since most of the novel concerns people's thoughts
rather than surface actions. These thoughts connect to people and
things far beyond the people and things that are ostensibly closest to
them.

Clarissa told Peter of this transcendental theory while riding on
an omnibus with him through London. The omnibus, an open-air
bus that offers a view of everything around, symbolizes the ease
with which the friends could once share their deepest thoughts. As
adults, they are restricted by the repressive rules of English society,
which is symbolized by great and somber automobiles with their
blinds drawn. Clarissa still believes in the interconnectedness of
humans and the natural world, and she thinks about it during her
walk to the shops. However, Peter and Clarissa no longer feel so
easy sharing their most deeply held ideas with one another, and
Peter supposes Clarissa has hardened into a boring and shallow
upper-class society wife who would no longer consider such ideas
true or important.

5. She felt somehow very like him—the young man who had killed himself. She felt glad that he had done it; thrown it away. The clock was striking. The leaden circles dissolved in the air. He made her feel the beauty; made her feel the fun. But she must go back. She must assemble.

This quotation occurs at the day's end, when Clarissa is at her party and receives news of Septimus's death from Lady Bradshaw. Clarissa retreats to the small room where the prime minister sat to reflect on the young veteran. She had never met him and does not even know his name, but she experiences a moment of clarity, or "moment of being," in the small room when she identifies strongly with him and his dramatic action. Woolf created Septimus as Clarissa's double, and throughout the book he has echoed her thoughts and feelings. In this scene, Clarissa realizes how much she has in common with this working-class young man, who on the surface seems so unlike her.

Everything converges in this one moment, and this scene is the climax of the book. The narratives of Clarissa and Septimus finally meet. A wall separates the public sphere of the party from Clarissa's private space, where her soul feels connected to Septimus's soul. The clocks that have been relentlessly structuring the passing day continue to chime. Despite the sounding clocks and the pressures of the party outside, however, Clarissa manages to appreciate that Septimus has preserved his soul through death. Clarissa began her day by plunging metaphorically into the beautiful June morning, and Septimus has now literally plunged from his window. An effort and commitment to the soul is necessary to plunge into life or death, and Clarissa, who has reached middle age and is keenly aware of the compromises she has made in her own life, respects Septimus's unwillingness to be crushed by an oppressive power like the psychiatrist Sir William. Clarissa repeats the line from *Cymbeline*, "Fear no more," and she continues to endure. She will go back to her party and "assemble." In the postwar world, life is fragmented and does not contain easy routes to follow, but Clarissa will take the fragmented pieces and go on trying to make life up as best she can.

KEY FACTS

FULL TITLE
Mrs. Dalloway

AUTHOR
Virginia Woolf

TYPE OF WORK
Novel

GENRE
Modernist; formalist; feminist

LANGUAGE
English

TIME AND PLACE WRITTEN
Woolf began *Mrs. Dalloway* in Sussex in 1922 and completed
the novel in London in 1924.

DATE OF FIRST PUBLICATION
May 14, 1925

PUBLISHER
Hogarth Press, the publishing house created by Leonard and
Virginia Woolf in 1917

NARRATOR
Anonymous. The omniscient narrator is a commenting voice
who knows everything about the characters. This voice appears
occasionally among the subjective thoughts of characters. The
critique of Sir William Bradshaw's reverence of proportion and
conversion is the narrator's most sustained appearance.

POINT OF VIEW
Point of view changes constantly, often shifting from one
character's stream of consciousness (subjective interior
thoughts) to another's within a single paragraph. Woolf most
often uses free indirect discourse, a literary technique that
describes the interior thoughts of characters using third-person
singular pronouns (*he* and *she*). This technique ensures that

transitions between the thoughts of a large number of characters are subtle and smooth.

TONE

The narrator is against the oppression of the human soul and for the celebration of diversity, as are the book's major characters. Sometimes the mood is humorous, but an underlying sadness is always present.

TENSE

Though mainly in the immediate past, Peter's dream of the solitary traveler is in the present tense.

SETTING (TIME)

A day in mid-June, 1923. There are many flashbacks to a summer at Bourton in the early 1890s, when Clarissa was eighteen.

SETTING (PLACE)

London, England. The novel takes place largely in the affluent neighborhood of Westminster, where the Dalloways live.

PROTAGONIST

Clarissa Dalloway

MAJOR CONFLICT

Clarissa and other characters try to preserve their souls and communicate in an oppressive and fragmentary post–World War I England.

RISING ACTION

Clarissa spends the day organizing a party that will bring people together, while her double, Septimus Warren Smith, eventually commits suicide due to the social pressures that oppress his soul.

CLIMAX

At her party, Clarissa goes to a small room to contemplate Septimus's suicide. She identifies with him and is glad he did it, believing that he preserved his soul.

FALLING ACTION

Clarissa returns to her party and is viewed from the outside. We do not know whether she will change due to her moment of clarity, but we do know that she will endure.

KEY FACTS

THEMES

Communication vs. privacy; disillusionment with the British Empire; the fear of death; the threat of oppression

MOTIFS

Time; Shakespeare; trees and flowers; waves and water

SYMBOLS

The prime minister; Peter Walsh's pocketknife and other weapons; the old woman in the window; the old woman singing an ancient song

FORESHADOWING

At the opening of the novel, Clarissa recalls having a premonition one June day at Bourton that "something awful was about to happen." This sensation anticipates Septimus's suicide. Peter thinks of Clarissa when he wakes up from his nap in Regent's Park and considers how she has the gift of making the world her own and standing out among a crowd. Peter states simply, "there she was," a line he will repeat as the last line of the novel, when Clarissa appears again at her party.

KEY FACTS

Study Questions and Essay Topics

Study Questions

1. *"Fear no more the heat 'o the sun / Nor the furious winter's rages" is a quote from Shakespeare's play* Cymbeline. *The words are repeated or alluded to many times throughout* Mrs. Dalloway, *by both Clarissa and Septimus. What do the words mean, and why do Clarissa and Septimus repeat them?*

Clarissa Dalloway first reads the words from *Cymbeline* in a bookshop window when she sets out to buy flowers for her party, and their meaning is particularly significant in light of World War I. The lines are from a funeral dirge and suggest that death is not a thing to be feared, but rather it should be seen as a relief from the hard struggles of life. World War I has wrought devastation throughout England, and tragedy or the possibility of it is never far from people's thoughts. Clarissa, a middle-aged woman who is coming to terms with her own aging and eventual death, meditates on these lines throughout the day. The words foreshadow the death of Clarissa's double, the veteran Septimus, who repeats them before he commits suicide.

The lines from *Cymbeline* connect to the strong use of nature imagery that appears throughout the novel. The characters who are most connected to nature, such as Clarissa and Septimus, are also the most responsive to poetry and reflect about death and their place in the world most frequently. Both Clarissa and Septimus feel the importance of fire. The "heat o' the sun" can appear as something wonderful, like passion. Clarissa describes romantic love as "a match burning in a crocus." The heat can also consume, however, and Septimus, mentally wounded by the horrors of war, feels that the world will erupt in flames, in a fire that can no longer be contained. Whether wonderful or deadly, the heat of the sun is constant, and something everyone must endure. The quote suggests that death be embraced as a release from the burden of endurance.

2.   *Woolf created Septimus Warren Smith as a double for Clarissa. In what ways are Clarissa and Septimus different? In what ways are they the same?*

Woolf originally planned to have Clarissa die at the end of *Mrs. Dalloway*, but she decided instead to create a double for her, Septimus Warren Smith. Septimus would die in Clarissa's place, while Clarissa continued to endure. Many obvious differences exist between the two characters. Septimus is a man and twenty years younger who has fought and been damaged in the war. Clarissa is of the upper class, while Septimus is a working-class clerk. Clarissa still finds meaning in the symbols of English society, such as the prime minister and expensive cars, while Septimus sees them as meaningless. While Clarissa is able to gather her face into a neat diamond shape so she can meet the world with pursed lips and an unflappable demeanor, Septimus's lips are loose and he has lost the ability to focus or distinguish reality from his own visions. Septimus's inner world overflows into the public sphere, whereas Clarissa's interior remains contained. Septimus is considered insane, while Clarissa remains sane.

Clarissa and Septimus differ, but they also share many physical and emotional qualities. Each has a beak-nose, enjoys being at home in the domestic sphere, and quotes Shakespeare. Both have doting spouses. The first time we encounter Septimus, he is observing the car that backfires, just as Clarissa is. Their similarities also go beyond these surface details. Both have an instinctive horror of those who crave power, such as Sir William and Miss Kilman. Both Clarissa and Septimus believe that people are connected to trees in a spiritual way, and nature matters a great deal to both of them. At the end of the novel, in a very direct link, Clarissa "felt somehow very like him—the young man who had killed himself." She realizes that Septimus's death is, like her party, an attempt to communicate. This moment is an epiphany, or moment of being, when Clarissa realizes that Septimus is in some way a part of herself.

3.   *Conversion is seen as a constant threat in the novel.*
      Which characters wish to convert others, and what are
      they trying to convert others to? Are some characters
      more susceptible to conversion than others?

The two characters who try most actively to convert others in the novel are the psychiatrist, Sir William Bradshaw, and Elizabeth's history teacher, Doris Kilman. Sir William ostensibly attempts to convert people to his conception of health and science, while Miss Kilman introduces people to her views on religion and God. Both characters, however, seek dominion over others and use the concept of conversion only to gain power. Miss Kilman admits to herself that it is Clarissa's soul she wishes to "subdue" and "make feel her mastery." Miss Kilman seeks power in the name of Christianity, just as Sir William exiles people to mental institutions in the name of science.

The very sight of Sir William makes Clarissa uncomfortable, and she is highly sensitive to his desire to convert people to his worldview. Her awareness and vulnerability to Sir William's and Miss Kilman's greed for power comes from her ability to think deeply and empathize with others' emotions and motivations. Septimus also has this acute awareness about the world around him, and he is even more susceptible to conversion than Clarissa, due to his low social status. English society is another force that tries to convert people, but it also, to some extent, protects the upper class from the control of someone like Sir William. While Lady Bradshaw succumbs to social—and marital—pressure, Lady Bruton, in contrast, is safe from Sir William's clutches due to her close association with the empire. She may have lost her sense of "proportion" with her Canada obsession, but other members of her class will indulge and protect her. Characters who are more individual, like Clarissa and Septimus, are more at risk than those who view themselves purely as part of English society.

SUGGESTED ESSAY TOPICS

1. MRS. DALLOWAY *is constructed from many different points of view, and points of view are sometimes linked by an emotion, a sound, a visual image, or a memory. Describe three instances when the point of view changes and explain how Woolf accomplishes the transitions. How do the transitions correspond to the points of view being connected?*

2. *Flowers, gardens, and nature are important motifs in the novel. Choose three characters and describe their relationships to the natural world. What do these relationships reveal about the characters or their functions in the novel?*

3. *Characters in the novel come from a range of social classes. What does Peter mean when he feels the "pyramidal accumulation" that weighed on his generation is shifting? How did the old social order weigh particularly heavily on women?*

4. *What role does Sally Seton play in Clarissa's life, and what is the significance of her surprise appearance at the party?*

5. *World War I affected all the characters in the book to some degree. How did the war influence at least three of the characters?*

6. *The multitude of minor characters in the novel can be compared to the chorus in a classical Greek drama. They are often observers in the street. Choose three or four minor characters and describe their roles. What is their importance to the novel as a whole?*

7. *When Clarissa reflects on Septimus's death at the end of the novel, she experiences a moment of being, or an epiphany. What truth becomes clear to her, and why is it significant?*

REVIEW AND RESOURCES

QUIZ

1. What does Clarissa set out to purchase in the novel's opening scene?

    A.   A bag of ice
    B.   Flowers
    C.   Champagne
    D.   Fairy lamps

2. What object does Peter Walsh always have with him?

    A.   A banjo
    B.   A flashlight
    C.   A silver comb
    D.   A pocketknife

3. What color is Clarissa Dalloway's party dress?

    A.   Lavender
    B.   Peach
    C.   Green
    D.   Red

4. In which month does the novel take place?

    A.   June
    B.   October
    C.   December
    D.   April

5. Which male character proposes marriage to Clarissa and is refused?

    A.   Hugh Whitbread
    B.   Septimus Warren Smith
    C.   Joseph Breitkopf
    D.   Peter Walsh

6. Septimus feels human nature is essentially evil. Which character does he claim embodies "human nature"?"

    A. Lucrezia

    B. Richard Dalloway

    C. Dr. Holmes

    D. Doris Kilman

7. Which line from a Shakespearean play is repeated several times throughout the novel?

    A. "Out, damned spot! Out, I say!—"

    B. "Fear no more the heat o' the sun / Nor the furious winter's rages"

    C. "If music be the food of love, play on"

    D. "But, soft! what light through yonder window / breaks?"

8. What is Lucrezia Smith's profession?

    A. Schoolteacher

    B. Cellist

    C. Hat-maker

    D. Florist

9. Septimus goes to the doctor because he is suffering from what illness?

    A. Shell shock

    B. A toothache

    C. Back problems

    D. The flu

10. Why does Lady Bruton invite Richard Dalloway and Hugh Whitbread to her home for lunch?

    A. She wants their advice on redecorating the parlor

    B. Richard and Hugh keep her in stitches with their crazy senses of humor

    C. She wants their help writing a letter to the editor concerning emigration to Canada

    D. She wants to warn them about Peter Walsh's arrival in the city

11. When Richard returns from having lunch at Lady Bruton's, what does he bring home to Clarissa?

   A.   A little chow dog
   B.   A bouquet of roses
   C.   A fountain pen
   D.   A Jacobean mug

12. Who does Clarissa compare herself to when she returns home to her attic room?

   A.   A marathon runner
   B.   A princess
   C.   A prisoner
   D.   A nun

13. What was the most exquisite moment of Clarissa's life?

   A.   When she got married
   B.   When she met Hugh Whitbread in the street
   C.   When Sally Seton kissed her on the lips
   D.   When Elizabeth agreed to wear her pink dress to the party

14. Where does Peter Walsh live?

   A.   Boston
   B.   India
   C.   London
   D.   Sweden

15. Where did Clarissa spend her summers as a girl?

   A.   Bourton
   B.   Edinburgh
   C.   Milan
   D.   Calcutta

16. What is the name of Peter's fiancée?

   A.   Marigold
   B.   Lily
   C.   Lucy
   D.   Daisy

17. What does Clarissa have in her hands when Peter Walsh makes an unexpected visit?

    A.   A tambourine
    B.   Scissors
    C.   A book
    D.   A spatula

18. What illness has Clarissa recently recovered from?

    A.   Influenza
    B.   Measles
    C.   A nervous breakdown
    D.   Typhoid

19. When Peter Walsh falls asleep in Regent's Park, what does he dream about?

    A.   A solitary traveler
    B.   A giant squid
    C.   His mother's handbag
    D.   An exam

20. Whom does Septimus hear speaking to him from behind trees and screens?

    A.   Mrs. Filmer
    B.   Lucrezia
    C.   Clarissa Dalloway
    D.   Evans

21. What does Sir William Bradshaw, one of Septimus's doctors, believe in most strongly?

    A.   Yoga
    B.   God
    C.   Proportion
    D.   A protein diet

22. Who does Clarissa see twice in the window across from her own?

   A. A calico cat
   B. An old woman
   C. Septimus Warren Smith
   D. A young man smoking a pipe

23. Where does Doris Kilman go after having tea with Elizabeth?

   A. Regent's Park
   B. Westminster Abbey
   C. Clarissa's house
   D. The Salvation Army shop

24. Which shocking action did Sally Seton take at Bourton?

   A. She smoked opium at dinner
   B. She brought a pony into the breakfast room
   C. She ran naked through the hallway
   D. She threw away all of Clarissa's father's books

25. What does Lady Bradshaw tell Clarissa at the Dalloways' party?

   A. That Septimus committed suicide
   B. That she's taking a holiday to Greece
   C. That Sir William has killed her soul
   D. That she would like a copy of Clarissa's punch recipe

SUGGESTIONS FOR FURTHER READING

BELL, QUENTIN. *Virginia Woolf: A Biography*. New York: Harcourt Brace Jovanovich, 1972.

BLOOM, HAROLD, ed. *Modern Critical Interpretations: Virginia Woolf's* MRS. DALLOWAY. New York: Chelsea House, 1988.

DOWLING, DAVID. MRS. DALLOWAY: *Mapping Streams of Consciousness*. Boston: Twayne, 1991.

LEE, HERMIONE. *Virginia Woolf*. New York: Alfred A. Knopf, 1997.

MARSH, NICHOLAS. *Virginia Woolf, the Novels*. New York: St. Martin's Press, 1998.

MEPHAM, JOHN. *Virginia Woolf*. New York: St. Martin's Press, 1992.

REINHOLD, NATALYA, ed. *Woolf Across Cultures*. New York: Pace University Press, 2004.

ROSENTHAL, MICHAEL. *Virginia Woolf*. New York: Columbia University Press, 1979.

SHOWALTER, ELAINE. "MRS. DALLOWAY: Introduction." In *Virginia Woolf: Introductions to the Major Works*, edited by Julia Briggs. London: Virago Press, 1994.

WOOLF, VIRGINIA. *The Common Reader*. New York: Harvest Books, 2002.

———. *Mrs. Dalloway's Party: A Short Story Sequence*. Edited by Stella McNichol. New York: Harcourt Brace Jovanovich, 1975.

ZWERDLING, ALEX. *Virginia Woolf and the Real World*. Berkeley: University of California Press, 1986.